my **revisi⏻n** notes

CCEA GCSE
LEARNING FOR LIFE AND WORK

Joanne McDonnell

HODDER
EDUCATION
AN HACHETTE UK COMPANY

pp. 3–4 *source A, questions 4 and 5* CCEA May 2011 GCSE Learning for Life and Work examination paper © CCEA 2011.

p.13 Vicious circle of prejudice diagram based on an idea by PlayBoard.

Although every effort has been made to ensure that website addresses are correct at time of going to press, Hodder Education cannot be held responsible for the content of any website mentioned in this book. It is sometimes possible to find a relocated web page by typing in the address of the home page for a website in the URL window of your browser.

Hachette UK's policy is to use papers that are natural, renewable and recyclable products and made from wood grown in sustainable forests. The logging and manufacturing processes are expected to conform to the environmental regulations of the country of origin.

Orders: please contact Bookpoint Ltd, 130 Milton Park, Abingdon, Oxon OX14 4SB. Telephone: +44 (0)1235 827720. Fax: +44 (0)1235 400454. Lines are open 9.00a.m.–5.00p.m., Monday to Saturday, with a 24-hour message answering service. Visit our website at www.hoddereducation.co.uk.

© Joanne McDonnell 2012
First published in 2012 by
Hodder & Stoughton Limited,
an Hachette UK company
338 Euston Road
London NW1 3BH

Impression number 10 9 8 7 6 5 4 3 2

Year 2016 2015 2014 2013

Cover photo © Paul Vismara/Stock Illustration Source/Getty Images

Typeset in Cronos MM Regular by Datapage

Artwork by Datapage

Printed and bound in Spain

A catalogue record for this title is available from the British Library

ISBN 978 1 444 15476 4

Get the most from this book

This book has been written to offer guidance, advice and helpful hints to enable you to achieve the best marks in your CCEA GCSE Learning for Life and Work examination (LLW). The book is divided into three areas of study, following the order and content requirements of the specification. These are:

1 Local and Global Citizenship
2 Personal Development
3 Employability

 Tick to track your progress

You can use the revision planner on the next two pages to plan your revision, topic by topic.

You can also keep track of your revision by ticking off each topic heading throughout the book. You may find it helpful to add your own notes as you work through each topic.

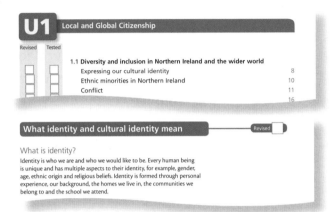

Features to help you succeed

What you need to know

A list of key revision points are given at the beginning of each topic, to target your revision.

Examiner tip

Throughout the book there are exam tips that explain how you can boost your final grade.

Key terms

Clear, concise definitions of essential key terms are provided for each topic. You should use this subject specific vocabulary in the answers to your exam.

Test yourself

Use these questions at the end of each topic to make sure that you have retained the key knowledge. Check your answers at **www.therevisionbutton.co.uk/ myrevisionnotes**.

Exam practice

Practice exam questions are provided for each topic. Use them to consolidate your revision and practise your exam skills. Go online at **www. therevisionbutton.co.uk/myrevisionnotes** to find sample answers for the practice exam questions.

Contents and revision planner

U3 Employability

Introduction

About the course

Learning for Life and Work is about preparing for what is ahead in your life. In adulthood we are faced with many decisions that will have an impact on our lives. This course is about providing knowledge and understanding to enable people to make informed decisions. It teaches you how to act responsibly and how to think independently.

Studying Learning for Life and Work will enhance many of your skills including managing information, problem solving, decision making, being creative, working with others and self-management.

The course is organised into three areas of study:

- Local and Global Citizenship
- Personal Development
- Employability

Centres are offered two specifications (your teacher will have chosen which you will study):

Specification A: Modular – five units in total

- **Units 1 and 2** – two controlled assessment tasks/reports: 30% each
- **Units 3, 4 and 5** – three 45 minute modular examinations, one for each of the three areas of study: 40%

OR

Specification B: Linear – three units in total

- **Units 1 and 2** – two controlled assessment tasks/reports: 30% each
- **Unit 3** – a one hour and 30 minute terminal examination covering all three areas of study: 40%

Guide to the modular exams

You will have a separate exam for each area of study. Each modular exam has two sections (Section A and Section B).

Section A

Section A is made up of three questions – you have to answer all of them. The questions ask you to demonstrate and apply your knowledge and understanding of the content that you have studied.

You should spend approximately 20 minutes answering the questions in this section. There are 20 marks available for Section A.

At the beginning of each question you are told the section on which the question is based. For example:

This question is from maximising and sustaining health and well-being

Each of the three questions is divided up into a further three parts, **(a)**, **(b)** and **(c)**. In order to achieve the maximum 20 marks you need to know what is expected of you in each question. The question stem (the beginning of the question) should guide you.

Question 1 (a) This part of the question is always worth **one** mark. It will begin with the question stem 'Name one' or 'Identify'. For example:

1 (a) Name **one** physical health problem caused by smoking. [1]

Your answer should be one sentence identifying the answer:

Smoking can cause lung problems.

One mark will be given for the correct answer.

Question 1 (b) and (c) These parts of the question are always worth **two** marks each. They will begin with the question stems 'Explain' or 'Identify and explain'. For example:

1 (b) Identify and explain **one** reason why employers should provide their employees with information about health and safety in the work place. [2]

Four lines will be provided for you to write your answer. You must make sure you identify **one** reason and then explain it:

An employer should explain health and safety because it is the law and so an employer can be taken to court if they do not provide this information.

One mark will be given for the identification (it is the law) and one mark for the explanation (employer can be taken to court if they do not provide the information).

Question 2 (a) This part of the question is worth **one** mark and takes the same format as question **1 (a)**.

Question 2 (b) and (c) These parts of question 2 are worth **two** marks each and will ask you to 'Explain' or 'Identify and explain' something. For example:

> **2 (b)** Explain **one** human right from the Universal Declaration of Human Rights. [2]

Four lines will be provided for your answer and it is important that you explain one human right and do not list other human rights:

> *One human right is a right to free education (article 26) and this means that every child has a right to go to school and that primary education should be free. In Northern Ireland every child from age 5 to 16 is entitled to go to school.*

You should answer the question in your explanation. Ask yourself the questions 'Have I shown the examiner I fully understand the human right to free education? Have I used connecting words?'

Question 3 (a) This part of the question is usually worth **two** marks and takes a similar format as questions 1(a) and 2(a), except that it will ask you to **name two** things. For example:

> **3 (a)** Name **two** types of friendship that a young person can have. [2]

In your answer, simply write down two types of friendship:

> *Pen pal and best friend*

Question 3 (b) and (c) These parts of question 3 are 'Explain' or 'Identify and explain' questions, the same style as in question 1 (b) and (c), except that they ask you to identify and explain **two** things. Each part is worth four marks.

Section B

Section B is made up of two questions (questions 4 and 5) – you have to answer both of them. These questions require more extended writing and your quality of written communication will be assessed in this part of the paper. This means your style of writing, spelling, use of grammar and punctuation must be of a high standard to score well. You should spend approximately 20 minutes answering the questions in this section. There are 20 marks available for Section B.

Inside the exam paper there will be an insert named 'Source A'. It is provided to help you answer both questions 4 and 5.

Source A

Young Entrepreneurs

Nowadays more and more young adults are setting up their own businesses and thus becoming entrepreneurs. Some of them work in the business on their own while others may employ people to work for them. Often the employer will provide training for their employees.

Entrepreneurs need to ensure that they are addressing various environmental issues, e.g. reducing, reusing and recycling waste materials, fuel emissions from vehicles, noise and air pollution and proper disposal of litter. They endeavour to become more socially aware by hoping to attract more customers as well as enhancing their corporate image. They are keen to use energy efficient measures to heat and light their premises in order to reduce electricity usage.

Question 4 (a) In this part of the question you are asked to **explain** two reasons/terms/laws. Each of these will be awarded two marks. A total of **four** marks are available. For example:

> 4 Read **Source A** and use it to help you answer this question.
>
>   **(a)** Explain **two** reasons why a business may need to employ new staff. [4]

> *(i) A business may need to employ new staff if employees within the business have been promoted and thus a vacancy may arise for a position to be filled.*
>
> *(ii) A business may need to employ more staff if the business has expanded and therefore more employees will be needed to cope with the workload.*

Question 4 (b) In this part of the question you must **use the source and your own knowledge** to help you explain something. For example:

> 4 Read **Source A** and use it to help you answer this question.
>
>   **(b)** Explain why an entrepreneur should be aware of environmental issues when setting up a new business. [6]

A maximum of **six** marks is available for this question and it is marked in levels from Level 1 to Level 3. It is important to use the source in your answer but more importantly you must develop this and offer more detail. Do not rewrite the source. You must show you understand what is written by explaining it.

> *An entrepreneur should be aware of environmental issues because it is something that some consumers look for when shopping for items. If a business is committed to environmental issues therefore, they may attract customers and this will result in more profit for the company. It will also attract prospective employees to the company as they may want to work for a company that is environmentally friendly. This could result in a more productive workforce. A business can enhance their corporate image by being environmentally friendly as this is regarded as a very respectable issue to be addressing. Also reusing and recycling can work out cheaper for businesses and so they could ultimately save money by being environmentally friendly.*

Your answer to this question must be detailed, clear and coherent, and should use specialist vocabulary.

> **Examiner tip**
> - Don't just copy points straight from the source.
> - Always develop any points you identify and ensure you give a full explanation.
> - Make sure you show a full understanding of what you are explaining in your answer.

Question 5 In this question you are asked to evaluate something with reference to the source provided. For example:

> 5 With reference to **Source A and your own knowledge**, evaluate the impact on the employer of providing training for their employees. [10]

> **Examiner tip**
> - This question asks you to evaluate. You must therefore give both the good and bad points.
> - Try to avoid writing in bullet points as this may prevent you from getting higher marks.

This question is worth **ten** marks. The answer will be judged in levels from Level 1 to Level 3.

Level 1 (1–4 marks)

The answer only focuses on a *few* positive *or* negative points. There is poor organisation and presentation, and a lack of clarity (it is unclear what the candidate is trying to say).

Example of Level 1 answer

> *If an employer trains the staff well this will be good for the business because they will know how to do the job better. An employee will be happy to have training because they will know how to do their job better and faster and this will keep the employer happy too.*

Level 3 (8–10 marks)

In this answer it is very clear that the candidate has a sound knowledge and understanding of the key issues to be argued. It also shows full awareness of the source. It is written with clarity and coherence (bullet points are not used). All points are fully explained and there is detailed analysis. The answer identifies, discusses, explains and analyses positive and negative points.

Example of a Level 3 answer

Training employees will greatly benefit an employer because it will mean that employees have up to date information and this will enable employees to carry out their job in an efficient manner. Well trained employees will be able to complete different tasks to a better quality and professionalism. This will lead to increased customers and sales for the employer. If an employee is given training they will feel valued and thus be loyal to the employer and so work more efficiently. On the other hand training can be expensive for employers and this can be a cost that many employers could do without to keep their business afloat. Also if an employee is trained this does not mean they will stay with that employer and could leave the job after training which would be a waste of money for the employer. This may be particularly true if employees are trained in sought after skills and qualifications. Training means time off the job and this can cost an employer money as indeed will be the cost of paying for a trainer or course for employees.

Remember that these questions are about how you use and analyse the information given.

Guide to the linear exam

You will have one exam, which will cover all three areas of study. The linear exam has three sections (Section A, Section B and Section C).

Section A

Section A is made up of three questions – you have to answer **all** of them. The questions ask you to demonstrate and apply your knowledge and understanding of the content that you have studied. You should spend approximately 25 minutes answering the questions in this section. There are 30 marks available for Section A.

Questions 1, 2 and 3 Part (a) of questions 1, 2 and 3 is worth **two** marks. This question begins with the question stem '**Name two**' or '**Identify two**'. Your answer should identify **two** things. See examples of these types of questions under question 3 (a) in the guide to the modular exams (see page 3).

Parts (b) and (c) of questions 1, 2 and 3 are worth **four** marks each. These begin with the question stem '**Identify and explain**'. Your answer should identify

and explain **two** things. See examples of these types of questions under question 1 (b) and (c) in the guide to the modular exams (see page 2).

> **Examiner tip**
> - Make sure you fully explain your answers – use connecting words (see page 3) to make sure you identify a point and then explain it.
> - Don't repeat the question stem. If you do this, you might forget to fully explain your answer.
> - Don't identify two separate points and make no explanation – you will only be awarded one mark.
> - Don't identify one point and then explain another – you will only get one mark.

Section B

Section B is made up of three questions (questions 4, 5 and 6) – you have to answer **all** of them. These questions require more extended writing and your quality of written communication will be assessed in this part of the paper. This means your style of writing, spelling, use of grammar and punctuation must be of a high standard to score well. You should spend approximately 25 minutes answering the questions in this section. There are 30 marks available for Section B.

Questions 4, 5 and 6 Inside the exam paper there will be an insert containing 'Source A', 'Source B' and 'Source C'. It is provided to help you answer questions 4, 5 and 6.

> **Examiner tip**
> - Read the sources on the insert carefully (at least twice).
> - Read the questions in Section B that the source relates to.
> - Read the source again and underline the relevant information to help you answer the questions.

Questions 4, 5 and 6 are made up of two parts: (a) and (b). A maximum of **four** marks is available for part (a) and **six** marks for part (b). Part (b) is marked in levels from Level 1 to Level 3. You can see examples of these types of question under question 4 (a) and (b) in the guide to the modular exam (see pages 3 and 4).

> **Examiner tip**
> - Don't just copy points straight from the source.
> - Always develop any points you identify and ensure you give a full explanation.
> - Make sure you show a full understanding of what you are explaining in your answer.

Section C

Section C is made up of three questions (questions 7, 8 and 9) – you have to answer **two** of them.

These questions require more extended writing and your quality of written communication will be assessed in this part of the paper. You should spend approximately 30 minutes answering the questions in this section, spending 15 minutes on each question. There are 20 marks available for Section C.

In each question you are asked to **evaluate** something with reference to the source provided. These questions are worth **10** marks each. The answer will be judged in levels from Level 1 to Level 3. See examples of these types of question under question 5 in the guide to the modular exam (see page 4). Examples of a Level 1 answer and a Level 3 answer are also provided.

Examiner tip

- This question asks you to evaluate and therefore you must give both the good and bad points.
- Try to avoid writing in bullet points as this may prevent you from getting higher marks.

Examiner tip

- If you answer all three questions, your best two answers will be used (the answers that scored the most marks). This is a very common error on the linear exam.
- Read the Chief Examiner's report for the exam you are about to sit – follow the Learning for Life and Work link on www.rewardinglearning.org.uk. This outlines all the common errors on the exam and gives advice for sitting the exam.

Countdown to the exams

6–8 weeks to go

- Start by looking at the specification – you can get this from the website (www.rewardinglearning.org.uk) or your teacher. Make sure you know exactly what material you need to revise and the style of the examination.
- Organise your notes, making sure you have covered everything on the specification. The revision planner (see pages iv–1) will help you to group your notes into topics. These *Revision Notes* organise the basic facts into short, memorable sections to make revising easier.
- Work out a realistic revision plan that will allow you time for relaxation. Set aside days and times for all the subjects that you need to study, and stick to your timetable.
- Set yourself sensible targets. Break your revision down into focused sessions of around 40 minutes, divided by breaks. Plan in little rewards for yourself when you have met your targets.

Revised ☐

4–6 weeks to go

- Read through the relevant sections of this book and refer to the examiner tips and key terms. Tick off the topics as you feel confident about them. Highlight those topics you find difficult and look at them again in detail.
- Test your understanding of each topic by working through the 'Test yourself' questions in the book. Look up the answers provided online at www.therevisionbutton.co.uk/myrevisionnotes.
- Make a note of any problem areas as you revise and ask your teacher to go over these in class.
- Look at past papers. They provide one of the best ways to revise and practise your exam skills. Write or prepare planned answers to the exam practice questions provided in this book. Take a look at the example answers provided online at www.therevisionbutton.co.uk/myrevisionnotes.
- Try different revision methods. For example, you can make notes using mind maps, spider diagrams or flash cards.
- Track your progress using the revision planner and give yourself a reward when you have achieved your target.

Revised ☐

One week to go

- Try to fit in at least one more timed practice of an entire past paper and seek feedback from your teacher, comparing your work closely with the mark scheme.
- Check the revision planner to make sure you haven't missed out any topics. Brush up on any areas of difficulty by talking it over with a friend or getting help from your teacher.
- Attend any revision classes put on by your teacher. Remember, he or she is an expert at preparing people for examinations.

Revised ☐

The day before the exam

- Flick through these *Revision Notes*.
- Check the time and place of your examination.
- Make sure you have everything you need – extra pens and pencils, tissues, a watch, bottled water, sweets.
- Allow some time to relax and have an early night to ensure you are fresh and alert for the examinations.

Revised ☐

My exams

Exam:

Date: ....
Time: ....
Location: ....

Exam:

Date: ....
Time: ....
Location: ....

Exam:

Date: ....
Time: ....
Location: ....

1.1: Diversity and inclusion in Northern Ireland and the wider world

Expressing our cultural identity

What you need to know:
- What identity and cultural identity mean
- The factors that influence a person's cultural identity
- The ways in which a person can express their cultural identity

Key terms

Bi-cultural – a society where there are only two cultural groups

Diversity – differences within a group or community

Multicultural – a society which is made up of a range of different cultural identities

Nationalist – one of the two main cultural/political groups living in Northern Ireland. Most Nationalists are from the Catholic community and wish to be politically linked to the Republic of Ireland

Unionist – one of the two main cultural/political groups who live in Northern Ireland. Unionists are usually from the Protestant community and believe in maintaining strong cultural/political ties between Northern Ireland and Great Britain

What identity and cultural identity mean

Revised

What is identity?

Identity is who we are and who we would like to be. Every human being is unique and has multiple aspects to their identity, for example, gender, age, ethnic origin and religious beliefs. Identity is formed through personal experience, our background, the homes we live in, the communities we belong to and the school we attend.

What is cultural identity?

Our cultural identity is what we share with members of a group. It is formed by the language, beliefs, values and customs of the society we come from.

Northern Ireland is a culturally diverse society, which means there are many cultures living here. Northern Ireland can no longer be viewed as bi-cultural (Nationalist/Unionist); it is, instead, a multicultural country. All of these different cultural groups express their cultural identity in a number of ways.

The factors that influence a person's cultural identity

Revised ☐

Each factor below has an influence on a person's cultural identity.

Factor	Examples of how it can influence a person's cultural identity
Family	Family values in the home Brought up within a particular religion Language(s) learned and spoken at home Musical influences from siblings
School	School values and mottos The sports played
Peer group	Friends wearing similar fashions Going out with friends to eat certain food Musical influences Going out to festivals or parades
Religion	Beliefs and morals from religion Traditional practices of certain religions
Media	Fashion trends shown in magazines Fashionable music or bands on TV or the radio
Community	Sharing with people in the same area the same political and religious beliefs

Examiner tip

You must be able to explain how these factors can influence a person's cultural identity.

The ways in which a person can express their cultural identity

Revised ☐

In Northern Ireland, people express their cultural identity in many ways.

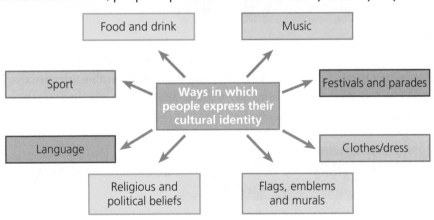

Food and drink · Music · Sport · Festivals and parades · Language · Clothes/dress · Religious and political beliefs · Flags, emblems and murals

Ways in which people express their cultural identity

Test yourself

Tested ☐

1 What are the factors that can make up your identity?

2 What are the factors that can influence your cultural identity?

3 What are the different ways that you can express your cultural identity?

Answers online

Exam practice

Tested ☐

Explain one way a person in Northern Ireland could express their cultural identity. *(2 marks)*

Answers online

Examiner tip

You must be able to explain how a person can express their cultural identity. Make sure you explain the point you make. A common error on this type of question is to identify a way in which a person can express their cultural identity but fail to explain *how* this expresses their cultural identity.

Ethnic minorities in Northern Ireland

What you need to know:
- How the population trend of Northern Ireland has changed
- The reasons why people have moved to Northern Ireland
- The opportunities and challenges of being a multicultural society

Key term

Ethnic minority – a cultural group which is not in the majority in a society. In Northern Ireland the largest ethnic minorities are from the Chinese, Indian, Pakistani, Polish and Eastern European communities

How the population trend of Northern Ireland has changed

Revised

There was some immigration into Northern Ireland in the 20th century, mainly from Asia, but the numbers of immigrants have increased markedly since 2004, especially from Poland, Lithuania, Czech Republic and Hungary.

As a result, today there are many different ethnic groups living in Northern Ireland: Chinese, Polish, Romanian, Lithuanian, Filipino and many more.

The reasons why people have moved to Northern Ireland

Revised

- Higher salaries are available in Northern Ireland compared to some other countries.
- UK-based employment agencies travelled to other countries, such as the Philippines and India, and offered the people who live there work in Northern Ireland.
- There is the potential to become self-employed.
- Northern Ireland has a better standard of living in terms of housing, education and health care than some other countries.

The opportunities and challenges of being a multicultural society

Revised

Many people believe that as a result of people from other cultures coming to live in Northern Ireland, and creating a multicultural society, the country is now presented with opportunities to become an enriched and more tolerant society.

However, some sections of our society disagree, and dislike the fact that people from other cultures are coming to live in Northern Ireland. This has led to some challenges.

Opportunities	Challenges
Promotes tolerance and understanding: When people from different cultural backgrounds live alongside each other in communities, they can learn about each other's cultures and share their different cultural experiences with each other.	**Can lead to a rise in community tension and racism:** Some communities may fear the movement of people from different cultural backgrounds into their society. People may attack other people from different cultural backgrounds.

Opportunities	Challenges
Can help to break down barriers: When people live alongside each other, they grow to understand that people from all different cultural backgrounds are human and deserve to be treated and respected equally. Ultimately, this leads to a society in which people respect one another.	**Can lead to prejudicial attitudes and stereotyping:** This can happen if people are not willing to be tolerant towards people from different backgrounds, or if people believe that their ethnic group is superior to another.
Brings diversity and vibrancy: It would be dull if everything was always the same. Northern Ireland is enriched with different festivals, languages, food, sports and music.	**Can lead to an increase in discrimination in the employment sector:** This can happen if people from different cultural backgrounds are prevented from accessing certain jobs or promotions.
Contributes to the economy: Skills and labour are brought to areas where there is a shortage (e.g. doctors, nurses and carers from India and the Philippines come to work in hospitals). New businesses are started, generating income and providing jobs for local communities. There is an increase in tax contributions.	**Puts pressure on resources and public services such as education, housing and health:** This is because of an influx of new citizens who need these services.

Test yourself

Tested ☐

1 Give one reason why people from different countries have decided to move to Northern Ireland.

2 List the opportunities for Northern Ireland as a result of people coming from other countries to live here.

3 What are the challenges that people from other countries bring to Northern Ireland?

4 For each challenge and opportunity you have written down, try to explain why this has happened. (Remember to use connecting words, see page 3.)

Answers online

Examiner tip

You should be able to identify and explain how the recent change in population trends has impacted on Northern Ireland, and you should be able to identify the positives (opportunities) and the negatives (challenges) of these changes.

Exam practice

Tested ☐

Evaluate the impact and contribution of new people from other countries coming to live in Northern Ireland.

(10 marks)

Answers online

Conflict

What you need to know:

● How expressions of cultural identity can lead to division and conflict

● The sources of conflict

● What sectarianism is

● What racism is and the laws concerning racism

● Examples of conflict in local, national and global areas

● The causes and consequences of prejudice, stereotyping, sectarianism and racism

● How individuals, society and government can combat sectarianism and racism

Key terms

Discrimination – treating someone unfairly because of the group they belong to

Prejudice – having inaccurate/irrational opinions about others and making judgements (pre-judging) about an individual or group without sound reason

Racism – believing or acting as though an individual or group is superior or inferior on the grounds of racial or ethnic origins, usually skin colour. This involves both racial prejudice and racial discrimination

Sectarianism – bigoted intolerance of other religious groups which can lead to prejudice, discrimination and violence between different religious groups

Stereotyping – having generalised views about a group and thinking that everyone in that group is the same, e.g. all football fans are hooligans

Examiner tip

Look at the key terms. The causes behind them, and the consequences that can happen because of them, are generally the same for each term (see the lists on page 14). Practise answering questions that ask for the causes or consequences of prejudice, stereotyping, sectarianism and racism.

How expressions of cultural identity can lead to division and conflict

Revised

People like to express their cultural identity as it gives them a sense of belonging to a group or a sense of solidarity. For some people, expressions of cultural identity such as language, sport or flags (see below) are threatening, especially when one group views itself as superior to another group.

In Northern Ireland, there is conflict between the two main cultural groups, the Unionist/Protestant and the Nationalist/Catholic – both have their own expressions of cultural identity based on their religious and political views. In Northern Ireland, most Catholics are nationalistic in their political view, whereas most Protestants consider themselves to be British.

Religious and political conflict is not a problem unique to Northern Ireland (see the table on page 14). There is evidence of it around the world. In the Middle East, for example, there is conflict between the Jews in Israel and the Muslims in Palestine over land they both feel they have a right to own.

Because cultural differences can sometimes be linked to political or religious views, expressions of cultural identity can cause tension when people strongly disagree with a particular group's belief.

A lack of understanding and respect for different identities and views can lead to conflict: attacks and tensions, stereotyping, sectarianism, prejudice and racism.

Flags demonstrate loyalty to a country. However, in Northern Ireland Nationalists identify with the Irish flag, while Unionists identify with the Union Jack. The flying of a particular flag can therefore cause conflict.

Marching can be seen as another source of conflict. Some people view parades as a part of their cultural identity, providing them with a sense of belonging. However, others perceive them as undermining their own particular identity.

The sources of conflict

Revised

- **Different religions** – Catholic, Protestant, Muslim, Jew, etc.
- **Different political beliefs** – Nationalist, Unionist, Republican, Loyalist, Socialist, Conservative, Communist
- **Different cultural practices** – food preparation, wearing traditional clothing
- **Different races**
- **Different ethnic backgrounds**.

Examiner tip

If an exam question asks about sources of conflict, give an answer using one of the sources here – stick to using the specialist vocabulary taught in citizenship.

What sectarianism is

Revised

One source of conflict is religious beliefs. Bigoted intolerance of other religious groups is called sectarianism. Northern Ireland has suffered from sectarianism for many years. It has become part of an attitude and behaviour that is being passed on by generations of families and is rooted in centuries of conflict and mistrust between Nationalists/Catholics and Unionists/Protestants.

The law on sectarianism

- **Fair Employment and Treatment Order (1998)** makes it unlawful to discriminate against someone on the basis of religious belief or political opinion.

- **Section 75 of the Northern Ireland Act (1998)** promotes equality between certain groups, e.g. those of different religious beliefs and political opinions.

What racism is and the laws concerning racism

Revised

Racism is the belief that one group of people should be treated less favourably than another, usually because of their skin colour. The diagram below shows how prejudice can lead to racism and discrimination.

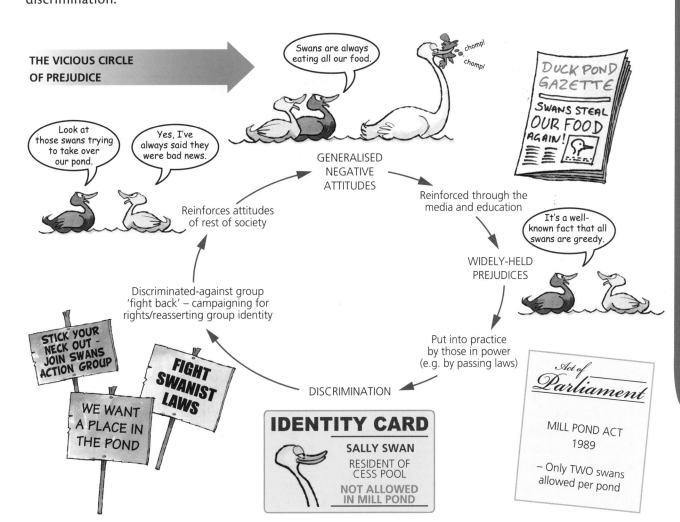

The law on racism

- **Race Relation Order (1997)** makes it illegal to discriminate on the grounds of race. This law also prohibits people from inciting racial hatred or being involved in any activity that could result in racism.
- **Section 75 of the Northern Ireland Act (1998)** upholds equality for all. This law means that it is compulsory for government authorities and other public bodies to actively promote equality and specifically points to promoting equality between racial groups.

Examiner tip

You will be expected to be able to identify the legislation that prohibits different types of discrimination.

Examples of conflict in local, national and global areas

Revised

Conflict can occur on various scales. It can take place within communities (e.g. rioting) or it can affect a whole country (e.g. war). The table below gives examples of how racism, sectarianism and different political beliefs have given rise to conflict in different areas – local, national and global.

	Local – your surrounding areas	National – the whole country	Global – the world
Racism	Towards Polish and Romanians groups	Towards Chinese people	Between people of different skin colour
Sectarianism	Between Catholics and Protestants	Between Catholics and Protestants	Between Muslims and Christians
Different political beliefs	Between Nationalists and Unionists	Between Conservatives and Labour	Between communist countries and democratic countries

The causes and consequences of prejudice, stereotyping, sectarianism and racism

Revised

Causes

- Lack of understanding and respect; ignorance and lack of education – this can lead to people having views that are unfounded.
- Segregated housing and education – although this is done to protect warring sides, it also results in there being very few opportunities for the two sides to mix. This prevents them from getting to know one another, breaking down barriers and moving away from prejudice, racism or sectarianism.
- The effects of the past (in Northern Ireland this relates to centuries of conflict and mistrust since the Plantation) – sectarianism is kept alive by those generations in each community that have been hurt through 'The Troubles'.
- Influence of family and friends – sectarianism, racism, prejudice and stereotyping may be an attitude or behaviour which is learned from other generations within a family or as a result of peer pressure.

Consequences

- Prejudice, stereotyping, sectarianism and racism can lead to hatred of different cultural and ethnic groups.
- This hatred can fuel violent criminal attacks on people and property, leading to vandalism, severe injury and even death in some cases.
- Victims can be intimidated.
- Victims can be discriminated against when using public services or in the workplace.
- Victims can feel excluded from areas of society, for example school, for fear of facing discriminatory comments or attacks.
- Victims can feel lonely and depressed.
- The local economy can be affected if it becomes known that a city/town is highly racist or is plagued with sectarian violence; tourists will not want to visit and businesses will not want to open because customers will not want to go to those areas.
- It can put pressure on services, such as the police and the health sector, that look after victims of discriminatory attacks.

Examiner tip

You will be expected to be able to identify the causes and consequences of prejudice, stereotyping, sectarianism and racism.

How individuals, society and government can work to combat sectarianism and racism

Revised

What an individual can do	What society can do	What government can do
Promote inclusion; build positive relations; have respect.	Organise cross-community or youth clubs to work together to organise anti-racist/anti-sectarian initiatives in which people can participate, learn and share experiences.	Ensure schools have an inclusion policy.
Encourage friends and family not to be racist or sectarian – challenge inappropriate behaviour.	Organise cultural celebration events in the local community.	Bring racism and sectarianism on to the curriculum so that schools have to teach these issues to their young people.
Attend lessons about racism/sectarianism in the local youth club or in school.	Organise educational sessions in local community centres to highlight the causes and consequences of racism/sectarianism on a community.	Pass laws to make racism/sectarianism illegal.
Report racist/sectarian crimes to the police.	Report racist/sectarian crimes to the police.	Introduce tougher sentences for those who continue to act in a racist/sectarian way.
Sign a petition against racism/sectarianism.	Organise anti-racist/anti-sectarian initiatives targeted at young people.	Provide funding for organisations such as Belfast Conflict Resolution Centre (BCRC), the Community Relations Council (CRC) or Northern Ireland Council for Ethnic Minorities (NICEM).
Join an NGO (Non-Governmental Organisation) that works to combat conflict in communities.		
Participate in events that aim to raise awareness of the negative aspects of racism/sectarianism.		
Lobby your local Member of the Legislative Assembly (MLA).		

Test yourself

Tested

1 Define the following words: prejudice, sectarianism and racism.
2 Using the words 'threatening', 'superior', disagree', write a sentence(s) explaining why expressions of cultural identity can cause conflict and division.
3 In your own words, explain why some people may find the flying of flags threatening.
4 Give an example of how someone may stereotype others.
5 Identify three sources of conflict.
6 Name two laws that make it illegal to be racist in Northern Ireland.
7 Give an example of a local sectarian problem.
8 Give an example of a national difference in political beliefs.
9 Give an example of a global racist problem.
10 Give two reasons why a person may be sectarian.
11 Give two consequences of racism.
12 Give one action a person could take to combat sectarianism.
13 Give one action society, e.g. a youth club, could take to combat racism.
14 Give one action the government could take to combat sectarianism and racism.

Answers online

Exam practice

Tested

1 Explain one cause of racism. *(2 marks)*
2 Explain how an individual can help to combat sectarianism. *(6 marks)*

Answers online

Examiner tip

Always read the question carefully to see from what perspective you are being asked to write your answer.

Conflict resolution

> **What you need to know:**
> ● The options available to resolve conflict

Key term

Judicial system – the system of courts within a particular country where the law of that country is applied and interpreted. The judicial system is usually part of the wider criminal justice system within a particular country

The options available to resolve conflict
Revised

Option	Advantages	Disadvantages
Mediation This is informal negotiation with an independent, neutral, third party.	Each group is given the opportunity to explain its views and can listen to the other group's points of view.	One group may refuse to empathise or listen, and walk out.
Sanctions These are often used by governments to change the behaviour of another government without using violence. Examples are withholding aid or loans.	These are peaceful methods of trying to change a government's behaviour and can be a good way of opening up negotiation.	The citizens of the country may suffer as a result and become innocent victims of the conflict. Sanctions often do not result in immediate change.
Boycotts A government may use this method to punish another government economically by refusing to buy goods from or sell goods to that country.	They put pressure on a government to change, but do so in a non-violent way.	Another country may buy these products or supply products to the country being boycotted, making the boycott ineffective.
Judicial system The courts can help to resolve disputes by using the law.	The courts can resolve issues in a peaceful and constructive manner. There can be consequences for people who do not adhere to the orders of a court.	Often people do not turn up to court or ignore court orders and this can lead to further disputes.
International human rights instruments Governments sign these in order to protect their citizens' human rights.	These ensure governments shape laws to protect human rights. If a government does not follow the instruments, it can be taken to court.	In countries that have not signed human rights instruments, or that are run by dictators, there are still many examples of human rights abuses.
The United Nations (UN) The central aim of the UN is to preserve world peace and improve people's lives.	The UN can send peacekeeping forces into a country to solve disputes peacefully and tackle the causes of conflict.	Rulers of some countries do not want interference from the UN. UN forces can face attack from rebel groups which can lead to further conflict and fatalities.

Test yourself
Tested

1 What are the different methods of conflict resolution?

2 For each method, give an advantage and disadvantage of using that method.

Answers online

Exam practice
Tested

Identify and explain two methods of conflict resolution. *(4 marks)*

Answers online

Examiner tip

The following methods of conflict resolution will also be accepted on an exam paper:

● cross-community groups working together
● teaching and promoting tolerance in schools
● celebrating cultures and traditions
● sharing experiences by learning from each other and getting some understanding of how the other side feels

Promoting inclusion

What you need to know:
- Why an inclusive society is important
- How schools can promote inclusion
- How inclusion can be promoted in the community
- How inclusion can be promoted in the workplace
- Why tolerance is important in a multicultural society

Key terms

Inclusive – ensuring that everyone is included, regardless of their background or material circumstances

Tolerance – acceptance of other people's differences

Examiner tip

You must be able to explain why a more inclusive society would lead to people receiving their basic human rights. Remember that human rights outline that everyone should be treated in the same way (not excluded), everyone is equal (regardless of colour, sex, language, etc.) and everyone has the right to life and to live in freedom and safety.

Why an inclusive society is important

Revised

There are many actions that can be taken to make a more inclusive society where no one feels left out or excluded. A more inclusive society has less racism, sectarianism and discrimination, which results in less conflict. This in turn ensures everyone receives their basic human rights.

How schools can promote inclusion

Revised

Schools must ensure everyone is respected and included in all aspects of school life. Schools provide an excellent opportunity for students to learn the importance of accepting those who are different to themselves. Schools can promote inclusion in a number of different ways:

- **School inclusion policy** – sets out the school's targets and actions that the school will take to ensure all students are included in all aspects of school life
- **Anti-bullying policy** – sets out the actions a school will take to ensure everyone is respected and the process to deal with incidents of bullying
- **Cultural celebration days** – students get to experience and learn about other cultures
- **Special assemblies** – students get knowledge and understanding of cultural diversity and the importance of tolerance
- **Multicultural food in the canteen** – students with special diets have their needs met and students get knowledge of the food practices of other cultures, increasing their understanding
- **Lessons in classrooms** – teach students about and raise awareness of human rights
- **After school clubs** – provide opportunities for students to come together to share their culture, language or interests and thus gain a better insight into different cultures
- **Access for those with disabilities** – whether this is ramps for wheelchair access or the use of hearing aid systems, schools must make changes to the building and teaching to allow access for those with physical disabilities.

Examiner tip

You must be able to demonstrate an understanding of why it is important that schools promote inclusion. This means inclusion of those of different races and religions, those with physical disabilities and those with special educational needs.

How inclusion can be promoted in the community

Revised

Communities play an important role in helping shape how society thinks and for this reason it is very important that communities send out a message of tolerance. This can be done in different ways:

- **Local community groups** can organise talks to promote tolerance in order to educate and raise awareness of the need for inclusion.
- **Community events** can promote multiculturalism by allowing people get to learn about and experience other cultures and thus promote tolerance.
- **Youth groups** can organise events that educate young people about why it is important to be an inclusive society. These can encourage young people to be more tolerant.

- **Local councils** can fund local events that enable people to share cultures and traditions and thus allow them to share experiences and build understanding.
- **Community Relations Council** can play a role in bringing communities together to build positive relationships through a range of initiatives and public events. They also work to support victims of 'The Troubles' and of sectarianism, racism, stereotyping.

How inclusion can be promoted in the workplace

Revised

Laws govern the workplace in terms of making sure they are places that protect people from discrimination and promote inclusion.

Act	How it protects people from discrimination
Equal Pay Act 1970	Gives men and women rights to equal pay for an equal job.
Sex Discrimination Act 1975	Protects men and women from discrimination based on gender.
Disability Discrimination Act 1995	Gives disabled people rights in areas of employment and access to goods, facilities, services and premises.
Race Relations Order 1997	Makes it unlawful to discriminate according to colour of skin, race, nationality or ethnic origin.
Fair Employment and Treatment Order 1998	Makes it unlawful to discriminate according to religious belief or political opinion.
Northern Ireland Act (section 75) 1998	Focuses on equality for minority groups, making it illegal to discriminate and compulsory for government bodies to actively promote equality so that certain groups in society have access to exactly the same opportunities.

Examiner tip

You must ensure you know how these Acts protect people in the workplace from discrimination.

Inclusion in the workplace is also promoted in other ways:

- **Training** of staff enables the employer to provide knowledge and understanding of why it is important to be an inclusive workplace, which can lead to employees being more tolerant.
- **Inclusion policies** set out targets and actions to be taken to ensure all employees feel included and respected, which can ensure an ethos of respect in the workplace.
- **Disciplinary policies** clearly set out targets and sanctions if any member of staff participates in behaviour that may be deemed to be discriminatory to another member of staff. This can ensure employees are aware of the consequences of this behaviour, which might reduce incidents of discrimination.
- **Equal pay** for people who carry out the same work or duties promotes inclusion.

Why tolerance is important in a multicultural society

If humans are intolerant of each other's differences this leads to conflict, which then has negative consequences for individuals and society – violence, depression, loneliness and death.

Test yourself

1 List four ways in which a school could promote inclusion.
2 Give two ways in which a community could promote inclusion.
3 What is the law that makes it illegal to act in a racist way?

4 What is the law that makes it illegal to discriminate against someone because of their disability?
5 Give two ways in which a workplace could promote inclusion.

Answers online

Exam practice

Identify and explain one way a school could promote inclusion.   *(2 marks)*

Answers online

1.2: Rights and responsibilities regarding local, national and global issues

What is social responsibility?

What you need to know:
● What social responsibility means
● The ways that a young person can demonstrate social responsibility
● The tactics used by pressure groups
● The methods of active participation used to bring about change

Key terms

Direct action – activities that target individuals, groups or property in order to achieve political, economic or social goals

Indirect action – activities undertaken to achieve political, economic or social goals that do not target a particular person, group or place

Pressure groups – NGOs and charities that put pressure on the government to change their policies and practice

What social responsibility means

Revised

Social responsibility is when individuals and groups within society commit themselves to making a difference to the lives of others and have a genuine concern about the welfare of others. They take on the responsibility of making society a better place.

The ways that a young person can demonstrate social responsibility

Revised

Local	Sign petitions to show support for a particular cause.
National	Join a peaceful protest to demonstrate disagreement with decisions that the government is making or laws that are being passed.
Global	Volunteer to give up time to work for a charity or NGO. Often young people go abroad to help in poverty stricken countries.

You can also be socially responsible by contacting politicians to make them aware of specific issues, or donating money to charities that try to improve the lives of others.

As part of a school community or youth club young people can participate in activities that demonstrate social responsibility, for example by trying to improve local facilities, such as a play park. Groups or societies can do this by using methods such as lobbying local councillors or fundraising.

The tactics used by pressure groups

Revised

Joining a pressure group is another way to try to make a change. Pressure groups try to put pressure on the government to persuade them to consider their particular cause. Some examples of pressure groups are: Amnesty International, Greenpeace, Oxfam, Friends of the Earth.

The tactics used by pressure groups may involve indirect or direct action.

Indirect action	Direct action
• Lobbying governments • Running campaigns to raise awareness of issues • Collecting funds • Producing materials for schools to educate pupils about issues • Taking part in and organising demonstrations or marches • Organising publicity stunts	• Strikes • Sit-ins • Vandalism • Graffiti • Scaling buildings • Sabotage • Using explosives

The methods of active participation used to bring about change

Revised

Method	Advantages	Disadvantages
Volunteering	People can feel that they are contributing to improving the lives of others, which can be a very rewarding experience. Many charities would not be able to continue without the support of volunteers.	It can be expensive and time consuming for the volunteer.

Method	Advantages	Disadvantages
Contacting politicians	People can raise awareness of their issue and a politician may take an interest and pursue the issue. This is an excellent way of making local politicians aware of local issues.	It can be time consuming and frustrating trying to contact politicians who are very busy people. It takes perseverance to get your views heard.
Signing petitions	People can feel that in a small way they have expressed their view and supported a cause. It can be a very effective method of showing the government that a lot of people support a particular cause as the government should listen to the views of the people in a democracy.	It can be time consuming and a petition needs to be very well supported to get noticed as there are so many groups who use this tactic to get their issue heard.
Donating	Donating money allows people to feel they are contributing to improving the lives of others. Without funding from donations many charities would not be able to carry out their work.	The amount of money that is required is phenomenal; people often get fed up with charities asking for money. Charities have to invent new ways of trying to fundraise.
Joining a peaceful protest	This is an excellent way of allowing the government to see that a number of people are unhappy about a certain issue – a protest can often result in the issue being debated in parliament.	Unfortunately some protests end in violence which brings negative publicity to the group that is protesting. People often distance themselves from this violent behaviour, as it is not seen as socially responsible.

Test yourself

Tested ☐

1 How could a young person demonstrate social responsibility on a local level?

2 How could a young person demonstrate social responsibility on a national level?

3 How could a young person demonstrate social responsibility on a global level?

4 What are the methods of direct action?

Answers online

Exam practice

Tested ☐

Evaluate the methods of active participation in bringing about change.

(10 marks)

Answers online

The Universal Declaration of Human Rights (UDHR)

What you need to know:

● The historical context of human rights

● Articles from the UDHR

● The two key legal documents inspired by the UDHR

● The role of the government in protecting the human rights of their citizens

● The ways that human rights can be limited

The historical context of human rights

Revised ☐

The language of rights has a long history dating from the Magna Carta in 1215, but human rights were formalised following the atrocities of the Second World War. The Universal Declaration of Human Rights (UDHR) was adapted by the United Nations general assembly in 1948, but it is not a legally binding instrument. At that time, 48 governments around the world signed the UDHR. It was signed to protect people's rights and is a promise or commitment made by governments to safeguard human rights.

Examiner tip

You only have to have knowledge of certain articles in the UDHR. These are outlined on pages 23–26.

Articles from the UDHR

Everyone:

- is born free and should be treated equally.
- has the right to a home and medical care if they need it.
- has the right to live in freedom and safety.
- should be free from slavery.
- should have a fair trial.
- has the right to rest and leisure.
- has the right to go to school.
- has the right to marry.
- has the right to take part in government and vote.
- has the right to an adequate standard of living.

The two key legal documents inspired by the UDHR

These two treaties were inspired by the UDHR and are intended to protect individuals from state abuses. States are held responsible for their actions towards their citizens.

- **European Convention on Human Rights** Governments who signed this treaty in 1950 have a legal obligation to make sure that their citizens have the rights laid down within the treaty. In 2000 the **ECHR** became part of domestic law in the UK. It is called the Human Rights Act.

- **The United Nations Convention on the Rights of the Child** This treaty is a list of promises made by governments to young people under the age of 18. It is specially written for children and focuses on their rights. The UK signed the **UNCRC** in 1990.

The role of the government in protecting the human rights of their citizens

The government has three main methods of protecting the human rights of their citizens:

- **Communication** – through campaigns the government can encourage members of the public to take their responsibilities seriously.
- **Legislation** – the government can make laws to protect those who are disadvantaged.
- **Education** – through educating young people in schools the government can encourage its citizens to become involved in tackling social injustice.

The government works through several bodies to ensure human rights are protected. These bodies include:

- Northern Ireland Human Rights Commission (NIHRC)
- Police Service of Northern Ireland (PSNI)
- Health and Social Services
- Department of Education (DENI)
- the justice system, which protects individuals who feel their rights have been violated as they can take their case to court.

The ways that human rights can be limited

- The use of CCTV can be used to prevent crime. However, it can also be argued that it undermines people's right to privacy. It is important to remember that rights come with responsibilities. There is a responsibility to the safety of others and sometimes this may cause a conflict between human rights.
- The reading of prisoners' letters and the censoring of what they read can conflict with the right to privacy.

- The media (television, newspapers, etc.) have the right to freedom of expression. However, sometimes the media can violate a person's right to privacy. Sometimes courts are used to decide which right is more important – an individual's right to privacy or the media's right to freedom of expression. Usually the deciding factor is whether the publication of material is in the public interest or not.

Test yourself

Tested

1 When was the UDHR signed?
2 Is it a legal document?
3 Give the name of two human rights treaties that were inspired by the UDHR.
4 List the ways in which the government attempts to protect the human rights of its citizens.

Answers online

Exam practice

Tested

Explain how the government can protect the human rights of its citizens.

(2 marks)

Answers online

Articles of the UDHR

What you need to know:

- Article 3: Life, liberty and the security of the person
- Article 12: Interference with privacy, family home or correspondence
- Article 21: The right to vote
- Article 23: The right to work with equal pay for equal work
- Article 25: Adequate health and well-being for self and family
- The issues of poverty in Northern Ireland
- Article 26: Free education, at least at elementary/fundamental stages
- The responsibilities that accompany human rights

Examiner tip

You do not need to know the number of the article (e.g. Article 3) but if you are asked to name a human right you must use the correct wording. If you are asked to explain a human right you must try to use the specialist vocabulary you have been taught in citizenship.

Article 3: Life, liberty and the security of the person

Revised

What this right means

People should have the right to live in freedom and safety, that is, no one has the right to take another person's life or cause them any harm. It is also there to protect us from unlawful detention.

How the government works to protect this right for its citizens

- The government passes laws that make it illegal for anyone to violate the safety or freedom of an individual, e.g. Northern Ireland Act (1998) (Section 75) aims to protect minority groups from hate crime.

- The police force is used by the government to uphold the law in order to keep citizens safe.

- International treaties – governments across the world work together to ensure that everyone enjoys their right to safety and security by signing treaties.

Article 12: Interference with privacy, family home or correspondence

Revised

What this right means

The UDHR states that everyone has 'the right to be protected if someone tries to harm your good name, enter your house, open your letters or bother you or your family without good reason'.

The significance of this right in today's world

This protects a citizen's right to privacy, which is a good thing for citizens. However, there is often a conflict between this right and the right to freedom of expression. At times this right may be limited to ensure the safety of others.

Article 21: The right to vote

Revised

What this right means

The UDHR states that 'You have the right to take part in your country's political affairs whether by belonging to the government yourself or by choosing politicians who have the same ideas as you. Governments should be elected regularly and voting should be carried out in secret. You should get a vote and all votes should be equal.'

The significance of this right in today's world

In a democracy, voting is free, fair and regular. However, even within a democratic country some people say the methods of voting are unfair. If there are minority groups who are voted for, some voting systems will not allow these groups to gain seats and be represented. Another issue is that a number of people choose not to vote and this can mean that an election result does not truly reflect the views of all of society. Some countries, such as Australia, make it compulsory to vote.

How we vote in Northern Ireland

In Northern Ireland, all men and women over the age of 18 can choose to vote. The voting system used is called proportional representation. This means that the percentage of votes that a political party receives will result in the percentage of seats they receive. Voters choose their candidate in order of preference using a system called Single Transferable Vote.

Article 23: The right to work with equal pay for equal work

Revised

What this right means

The UDHR states that people should have the right to work and to earn a salary which allows them to support their family. It also states that if a man and a woman do the same work they should receive the same pay.

The significance of this right in today's world

This means that everyone has the right to work. The government must put systems in place to support those not at work. This can often cause disagreement because some people choose not to work and to live off state benefits and many people do not think that these people should be supported.

How the government works to protect this right for its citizens

- Laws are used to govern the workplace to ensure the rights of citizens are protected. Some of these laws ensure equal opportunities to ensure all men and women can access the world of work and work safely in work. Some of this legislation is outlined on pages 27–28 and some in Unit 3: Employability, see pages 89–90.

- There is a responsibility on all employers to make sure they respect and uphold this right.

Article 25: Adequate health and well-being for self and family

Revised

What this right means

Adequate health and well-being refers to human needs such as: food, clothing, housing, medical care, necessary social services and security in the event of unemployment.

The significance of this right in today's world

This right is difficult to uphold as there is still evidence of poverty in Northern Ireland and around the world. This right also refers to social inclusion, which means that everyone should be included in society. In order to do this, special support should be given to those who need extra help.

The issues of poverty in Northern Ireland

Revised

What is poverty?

Poverty can be defined as relative or absolute poverty:

- **Relative poverty** – people do not have adequate income or resources, which prevents them from enjoying a standard of living that would be regarded as acceptable by society in general.

- **Absolute poverty** – people do not have the basic essentials such as food and shelter which they need to survive.

Living in poverty can lead to people feeling excluded, isolated, powerless and discriminated against.

What is the situation in Northern Ireland?

Various groups of people can be severely affected by poverty:

- **Homeless** – This does not only refer to people who sleep on the streets but also those who are living in homes that are unsuitable. It means not owning or renting your own home. NGOs like Shelter and the Simon Community provide long- and short-term aid to those experiencing housing problems. NGOs provide shelter and accommodation and work to tackle the problems that lead to homelessness.

- **Children** – In Northern Ireland there are children living in relative poverty, without material things and activities that their peers take for granted. Around the world many children are living in absolute poverty with no access to regular food or housing. NGOs fundraise to send volunteers and money to help those in poverty. They offer training and advice to people to help them escape the poverty trap.

- **Unemployed** – As seen in Article 25 of the UDHR, it is a basic right to be helped if you find yourself out of work. Unemployment can lead to poverty, stress, divorce and homelessness. The government offers various benefits, schemes and programmes that help people who are out of work and help get them back into work.

- **Elderly** – There is evidence that in the UK many pensioners are so poor they find it hard to heat the house, eat nutritious food or replace household equipment. The two main causes of poverty in the elderly are that they have an inadequate pension and do not claim the benefits to which they are entitled.

Article 26: Free education, at least at elementary/fundamental stages

Revised

What this right means

Every child has the right to go to school. Primary education should be free.

The significance of this right in today's world

In Northern Ireland it is compulsory to attend school from age five to sixteen. Local education authorities have a legal duty to ensure that free education is available to every child. Problems occur when children refuse to go to school or parents do not support the system. The government has people in place to offer support to these families and their children. In many developing countries children do not have access to free education.

The responsibilities that accompany human rights

Revised

Each of us has our human rights but we also have a responsibility to protect the human rights of others. Here are some examples of how rights carry responsibilities.

Human right	Key responsibility
Everyone is entitled to free education (Article 26).	We should support the systems in place and ensure children attend school.
Everyone is entitled to live in freedom and safety (Article 3).	We should treat everyone with respect and not do anything that would harm another individual.
Everyone has the right to work (Article 23).	Employers have a responsibility to provide work and a decent salary. Also we have a responsibility to attend work.

Test yourself

Tested

1 List the human rights articles that you need to know.
2 Beside each right, give its meaning in your own words.
3 Beside each meaning, explain how this right has had an impact on your life.
4 What is proportional representation?
5 What is Single Transferrable Vote?
6 What is relative poverty?
7 What is absolute poverty?
8 List the problems related to poverty in Northern Ireland.
9 What groups work to tackle these problems?
10 Why do human rights carry responsibilities?

Answers online

Exam practice

Tested

Explain one reason why a person's human rights may be limited by the government. *(2 marks)*

Answers online

1.3: The role of society and government in safeguarding human rights

The law

> **What you need to know:**
> - What equality means
> - The difference between treating someone equally and treating someone fairly
> - The laws relating to equal opportunities and discrimination
> - What Section 75 means
> - The groups of people who are more likely to be marginalised in society
> - The role of the Office of the First Minister and Deputy First Minister (OFMDFM) in promoting and protecting human rights

> **Key term**
>
> Marginalised – made to feel excluded or unimportant

What equality means

Revised

Equality means everyone should have the same opportunities in life and no one should be excluded from any aspect of social life. Therefore, everyone should have the same access to education, work, housing, leisure facilities, etc.

The difference between treating someone equally and treating someone fairly

Revised

Treating everyone fairly does not mean treating everyone equally. Sometimes you have to treat people differently to ensure they are being treated fairly. There are vulnerable groups in society who need more support and help than others, for example those who are homeless and living in poverty. By giving them more support, they are treated differently to other people, for example they are given help to get a house. This is to ensure they are not excluded from participating in any part of society and can have the same opportunities as everyone else. This is positive discrimination.

The laws relating to equal opportunities and discrimination

Revised

The laws shown in the table below protect people's rights and try to prevent discrimination.

Legislation	What does this mean?
Equal Pay Act 1970	This law gives men and women rights to equal pay and other benefits such as sick pay. It also states that a woman should not lose her job because of pregnancy.
Sex Discrimination Act 1975	This law was introduced to protect men and women from discrimination on the grounds of sex or marriage.
Disability Discrimination Act 1995	This law introduced new rights for disabled people in areas of employment and access to goods, facilities, services and premises.

Legislation	What does this mean?
Race Relations Order 1997	This makes it unlawful to discriminate against someone on the basis of colour, race, nationality or ethnic origin.
Fair Employment and Treatment Order 1998	This makes it unlawful to discriminate against someone on the basis of religious belief or political opinion.
Equality Act 2000	This law brought together the different equality legislation in a simpler form.

What Section 75 means

Revised

One of the most important equality laws in Northern Ireland is Section 75 of the Northern Ireland Act 1998. This law means that all public institutions, schools and other government organisations must make sure that certain groups who are likely to be marginalised in our society have access to the same opportunities as everyone else.

The groups of people who are more likely to be marginalised in society

Revised

The following groups of people may be more likely to face exclusion because they are seen as different or face poverty and cannot access services:

- Those with a disability
- Those facing sexual discrimination – homosexual, bisexual
- Racial minorities
- Those facing gender discrimination.

The consequences for those who are marginalised in society can be discrimination, hate, crime, depression, fear and loneliness.

> **Examiner tip**
>
> You must be able to explain why exclusion from society may lead to the consquences outlined.

The role of the Office of the First Minister and Deputy First Minister (OFMDFM) in promoting and protecting human rights

Revised

The duties of the OFMDFM include:

- working with the Northern Ireland Human Rights Commission (NIHRC) to oversee and ensure all laws uphold human rights
- building good community relations in order to protect everyone's right to safety

- promoting equality of opportunity for all and tackling social disadvantage, e.g. poverty, in order to protect everyone's right to adequate health and well-being
- creating a more inclusive and equal society and thus tackling any instances of discrimination or violation of human rights.

The OFMDFM does this through:

- providing investment for community groups to tackle issues
- financing and organising media advertising campaigns to target social problems
- advising schools to educate on certain issues to try to solve problems such as discrimination.

> **Examiner tip**
>
> You must be able to fully explain how each of these duties can ensure the promotion and protection of society's rights.

Test yourself

1 What is equality?
2 Explain the difference between equality and fairness.
3 List two laws relating to equal opportunities or discrimination.

4 What does Section 75 mean?
5 What are the consequences for groups of people who are marginalised in society?
6 List the duties of the OFMDFM regarding protecting human rights.

Answers online

Exam practice

Tested

Explain the role of the government in protecting the human rights of their citizens. *(2 marks)*

Answers online

1.4: Non-governmental organisations (NGOs)

The role and contribution of non-governmental organisations (NGOs)

What you need to know:
- What social justice means
- The causes and consequences of social injustices
- Examples of non-governmental organisations

What social justice means

Revised

Social justice is about every one of us having the opportunity to make the most of our lives and use our talents to the full. It also refers to opportunities to ensure that social issues and problems such as unemployment, poverty and homelessness do not get any worse in society. It focuses on building a society that is based on equality and values human rights.

The causes and consequences of social injustices

Revised

Causes	Consequences
• The widening gap between the rich and poor	• Poverty
• Unequal distribution of resources	• Low life expectancy
• Discrimination	• Malnutrition
• Undemocratic leaders	• Homelessness
• Poor education	• High infant mortality rates
• Bad housing	• Poor health
• Low incomes	

Examples of non-governmental organisations

NGOs do not receive any money from the government and so have to do their own fundraising. They are charities that deal with social injustices.

The Northern Ireland Council for Voluntary Action (NICVA)

History	Began in 1938 in response to high levels of unemployment. Became known as NICVA in 1986.
Issues it deals with	Represents the entire voluntary and community sector in Northern Ireland, providing organisations with support and advice on how to run successfully.
How it addresses such issues	Provides specialist training programmes for organisations; gives specialist advice on fund-raising, training and management; issues a magazine and bulletin; advises on charity law.
How society can play a part	By supporting voluntary and community groups – through using the services of a voluntary organisation or helping fundraise for an organisation. People can also fundraise for NICVA or offer their time if they have expertise in a certain area.
How the government can play a part	By supporting the work of NICVA through financial support or promoting its work.
Current projects	Working with a variety of voluntary groups such as Gingerbread, Homeless NI, Youthnet.
Effectiveness	It is making a positive contribution by protecting and supporting voluntary and community groups that may not be able to sustain their work without the help of NICVA.

Amnesty International

History	Formed in 1961 on the belief in the power of ordinary people to make extraordinary change.
Issues it deals with	Protecting people wherever justice, fairness, freedom and truth are denied.
How it addresses such issues	It is a campaigning NGO, therefore it organises mass protests and lobbies governments to make change.
How society can play a part	By joining as a member, donating money, fundraising, shopping in its charity shops, becoming a volunteer, getting involved with an Amnesty International youth group or community group or campaigning on own area of interest.
How the government can play a part	By supporting its work through pressurising other bodies that uphold justice and educating young people about the work of Amnesty International.
Current projects	Fighting deep poverty; women's rights; supporting change in the Middle East and North Africa; campaigning against torture and ill treatment in Egypt and Syria.
Effectiveness	It is now a global movement with over 3 million supporters. It has made incredible changes to the lives of many citizens of countries that have been denied their rights.

Friends of the Earth

History	Founded in 1969 in the USA and became an international organisation in 1971.
Issues it deals with	Environmental and social issues: works to create a healthier environment for all.
How it addresses such issues	Campaigns, lobbies and challenges the government; organises rallies and protests; works with communities to inspire solutions to problems.
How society can play a part	By donating time or money or indeed just living an environmentally friendly lifestyle.
How the government can play a part	By passing legislation that it is campaigning for; educating young people in schools how to be more environmentally friendly; supporting the message of being environmentally friendly and communicating that this is the best way forward for the earth.
Current projects	Global warming; how to make homes energy efficient; reduce deforestation; halving the waste that is thrown away; calling for councils to tackle climate change.
Effectiveness	Friends of the Earth has been very successful in getting governments to legislate on a number of issues including banning whaling.

Oxfam

History	Founded in 1942 to tackle famine, it now is a worldwide charity and development agency.
Issues it deals with	Emergency relief; development work; campaigning for change.
How it addresses such issues	Provides immediate short-term aid in countries where there is war or has been a natural disaster; working directly with communities to help them become self supporting; lobbying governments to bring about change to end poverty and injustice around the world
How society can play a part	By donating time and money to any of the projects that Oxfam is working on and shopping in their charity shops.
How the government can play a part	By passing legislation and putting pressure on other governments to make changes by communicating Oxfam's message and educating young people in schools about the work of Oxfam and how they can be supported.
Current projects	Brazil – improving access to clean water supplies; Pakistan – providing emergency relief after the floods; East Africa – appeal to give aid to those in the food crisis.
Effectiveness	Oxfam has been hugely successful in changing people's lives around the world for the better. Many people owe their lives to the people who work voluntarily for Oxfam.

War on Want

History	Formed in 1951 to fight poverty. The then future Prime Minister Harold Wilson coined the name.
Issues it deals with	Highlighting the needs of poverty stricken countries and fighting the root causes of poverty not just the effects; targeting sweatshops and plantations, food justice, conflict zones.
How it addresses such issues	Lobbies governments and international agencies to tackle problems of poverty; supports workers to achieve their human rights; supports small farmers who are being pushed out by multinational agribusiness; works with people in war zones to make sure they can protect themselves against human rights abuses.
How society can play a part	By donating time and money or by shopping in their stores.
How the government can play a part	By putting pressure on other governments to bring about change that will reduce instances of poverty; educating and communicating the messages of War on Want.
Current projects	Fighting supermarket power; stopping the 'business' of war, for example private armies; trade justice; sweatshops; justice for Palestine; tax not cuts.
Effectiveness	This NGO has led ground-breaking campaigns and is at the forefront of the trade justice movement. It was also a key player in the Make Poverty History campaign.

Save the Children

History	Established in the UK in 1919.
Issues it deals with	Improving the lives of children around the world and ensuring they have access to proper food, healthcare, education and protection.
How it addresses such issues	Runs development programmes to help children and families help themselves; provides on-the-ground support in areas where there has been conflict or a natural disaster; campaigns for children's rights.
How society can play a part	By donating or volunteering to work for Save the Children.
How the government can play a part	By upholding and promoting children's rights; by putting pressure on those governments that need to improve the lives of the children in their country.
Current projects	Haiti earthquake; East Africa appeal.
Effectiveness	This NGO is really making a difference in the UK and abroad, enabling more children to access education and get basic vaccines.

Test yourself

Tested ☐

1 What is social justice?
2 Name three examples of social injustice.
3 Name three causes of social injustice.
4 Name three consequences of social injustice.
5 List three things you have learned about each NGO.

Answers online

Exam practice

Evaluate the different ways that NGOs can tackle a global issue such as poverty.

(10 marks)

Answers online

1.5: Key democratic institutions and their role in promoting inclusion, justice and democracy

What do we mean by democracy?

What you need to know:
- What democracy means
- The different types of democracy
- The key characteristics of a democracy
- The features of a non-democratic state

What democracy means

Revised

The word 'democracy' comes from the Greek language:

Demos = common people   *Kratos* = strength or power.

The word literally means strength or power of the people. Today a democratic state or organisation is one in which the ordinary people have a say in how it is run. Democracy is often associated with freedom and rights, such as the right to vote.

The different types of democracy

Revised

Direct democracy

- This is when each person casts their own vote.
- In Switzerland and in a number of states in America, they have referenda and town meetings so that everyone can have their say.
- People in Northern Ireland had a direct say in the Good Friday Agreement in 1998, with 71 per cent voting 'yes' to a devolved government of Northern Ireland.

Representative democracy

- This is when we elect someone to act on our behalf, such as a Member of the Legislative Assembly (MLA), Member of Parliament (MP), Member of the European Parliament (MEP) or a local councillor.

The key characteristics of a democracy

Revised

Characteristic	Explanation
Participation rights	There is equality and fairness for all citizens regardless of race, religion, gender, political opinion, etc., thus human rights are enjoyed by all citizens.
Elected government	Elections are held which are free and fair. The elections give citizens a chance to voice their opinion and participate. Elections must be regular (every 4–5 years). There are different types of elections – general (national), local (for councils) and referenda (votes on a single issue).

Characteristic	Explanation
Party system	There is a multi-party system where there is more than one political party to choose from.
Accountability of government	There is transparency and openness in how the government is run.
Constitution	There is a set of rules about how the country is to be run.
Freedom of expression	People can openly criticise the government, protest and voice different opinions.
Power, authority and the rule of law	The rule of law is obeyed, works effectively and has the best interests of the people at heart. Leaders use power responsibly. The police and courts are usually accepted by most citizens.

The features of a non-democratic state

Revised

- Citizens cannot voice their opinion.
- Citizens cannot campaign openly.
- Elections are controlled.
- The rights of the people may be denied.
- The press is controlled by the state.

Test yourself

Tested

1 Explain the term 'democracy'.
2 List the features of democracy.
3 What does it mean that elections must be free, fair and regular?
4 What is the constitution?
5 How can a government be accountable?
6 List the features of a non-democratic state.

Answers online

Exam practice

Tested

Identify and explain one feature of a democratic state.   *(2 marks)*

Answers online

The role of the Northern Ireland Assembly

What you need to know:

- What the Good Friday Agreement means to the people of Northern Ireland
- The role of the Northern Ireland Assembly
- The areas over which the Northern Ireland Assembly has power
- The responsibilities of the OFMDFM
- The role of the Executive Committee
- The role of a Member of the Legislative Assembly (MLA) in Northern Ireland
- The role of local councils

Key terms

Constituency – a voting area or region

Devolved government – a government with devolved (handed down) legislative powers

Legislative – law-making

What the Good Friday Agreement means to the people of Northern Ireland

Revised

The current democratic government in Northern Ireland was set up after the signing of the Good Friday Agreement between the British and Irish governments. This was an attempt by both governments to bring peace and democracy to Northern Ireland.

On 10 April 1998, the Good Friday Agreement was signed by the British and Irish governments. The agreement was endorsed in a referendum on 22 May 1998 when 71 per cent of voters supported the agreement. In the Republic, 94 per cent agreed to change their constitution in line with the agreement. This agreement was a major breakthrough in the peace process and for the people of Northern Ireland.

As a result, a devolved government of Northern Ireland was established which is committed to power sharing between the largest political communities. It means that local representatives make decisions that affect them. Local representatives usually have more understanding of the needs of the people within their part of the UK.

It was viewed by most people as an opportunity for the people of Northern Ireland to resolve their differences and move forward to a future of equality and peace.

The role of the Northern Ireland Assembly

Revised

The Northern Ireland Assembly is a legislative body, which promotes equality of opportunity for all citizens in Northern Ireland.

The Northern Ireland Assembly is made up of the Office of the First Minister and Deputy First Minister (OFMDFM), the Executive Committee and 108 Members of the Legislative Assembly (MLAs).

The areas over which the Northern Ireland Assembly has power

Revised

The Assembly has the power to make decisions on:	The Assembly does not have the power to make decisions on:
• Health	• Taxation
• Education	• Elections
• Agriculture	• National security
• Culture, arts and leisure	• War
• Regional development	• Space travel
• Social development	
• How the budget for Northern Ireland is spent	
• Supporting local business and bringing jobs to Northern Ireland	

The responsibilities of the OFMDFM

Revised

- Supporting the Executive Committee and liaising with the Assembly
- Supporting the North–South Ministerial Council, British–Irish Council, Civic Forum and UK departments
- Helping develop a programme for government and the Executive's economic policies
- Sustainable development
- Promoting and monitoring the implementation of equality of opportunity/good relations with the help of the NIHRC and the Equality Commission
- Tackling poverty and social exclusion, helping children and young people, supporting victims and survivors
- Review of public administration
- Emergency planning
- Improving investment in infrastructure.

The role of the Executive Committee

This is the name given to all the departments within the NI Assembly. Each department is run by a government minister who is an elected MLA (see below).

The eleven ministerial departments are:

1 Department for Employment and Learning
2 Department of Education
3 Department of the Environment
4 Department of Culture, Arts and Leisure
5 Department of Finance and Personnel
6 Department for Regional Development
7 Department of Enterprise, Trade and Investment
8 Department for Health, Social Services and Public Safety
9 Department of Agriculture and Rural Development
10 Department for Social Development
11 Department of Justice.

The role of a Member of the Legislative Assembly (MLA) in Northern Ireland

There are eighteen constituencies in Northern Ireland. Six MLAs are elected from each constituency, giving 108 MLAs in total. MLAs are elected by the people of Northern Ireland to represent them in the Northern Ireland Assembly. The MLAs meet every Monday and Tuesday for plenary sessions, which can involve debates and voting. These take place in Stormont buildings in Belfast. A speaker controls the meetings.

The role of local councils

Local councils deal with local everyday issues such as:

- leisure facilities
- waste collections
- licensing premises
- public health and safety
- registering marriages
- naming streets
- local events and festivals.

Members of the local council are called councillors. Local services are funded by 'rates', which are a property tax. The amount you pay is based on the house in which you live.

Test yourself

1 When was the Good Friday Agreement signed?
2 How was it endorsed by the people of Northern Ireland?
3 What does the agreement mean for the people of Northern Ireland?
4 What is the role of the Northern Ireland Assembly?
5 List four issues on which the Northern Ireland Assembly has the power to make decisions.
6 List three issues on which the Northern Ireland Assembly does not have the power to make decisions.
7 List five responsibilities of the OFMDFM.
8 What is the role of the Northern Ireland Executive?
9 How many constituencies are there in Northern Ireland?
10 How many MLAs are elected in Northern Ireland?
11 What is the role of an MLA?
12 List four issues that local councils deal with.

Answers online

Exam practice

Explain one of the roles of the Northern Ireland Assembly. *(2 marks)*

Answers online

Other institutions created under the Good Friday Agreement

> **What you need to know:**
> - The role of the Northern Ireland Human Rights Commission (NIHRC)
> - The role of the Police Ombudsman for Northern Ireland
> - The role of other institutions created under the Good Friday Agreement

The role of the Northern Ireland Human Rights Commission (NIHRC)

Revised

The NIHRC is an independent statutory body, not an NGO or a government body. It was established in 1999 as part of the Good Friday Agreement. Equality and human rights are fundamental in solving the conflict in Northern Ireland, and so the NIHRC was created to promote awareness of the importance of human rights.

The Commission works to ensure human rights are protected by:

- **advising government** on its obligation to uphold human rights
- **reviewing law and practice** to make sure they are in line with human rights standards
- **putting forward proposals for new laws** such as a Bill of Rights for Northern Ireland
- **investigating** matters of concern and conducting research into human rights issues such as prison conditions, mental health care and racism
- **promoting awareness** of human rights in, for example, schools and the police service by providing resources
- **taking cases to court** to highlight alleged human rights abuses
- **working with other organisations** to promote human rights in Northern Ireland.

The role of the Police Ombudsman for Northern Ireland

Revised

The Police Ombudsman for Northern Ireland was established under the Police (Northern Ireland) Acts of 1998 and 2000 to ensure a fair police system, in which the public can have confidence. It consists of professional investigators who gather evidence to show if the Police Service of Northern Ireland (PSNI) has acted inappropriately. In the past, these complaints were investigated by other police officers, which sometimes led to accusations of covering up.

The Police Ombudsman investigates complaints made about police officers relating to:

- use of force by police officers
- perverting the course of justice
- rude or offensive behaviour.

They also investigate:

- all discharges of firearms (including Taser)
- all fatal road traffic accidents involving police officers
- any death that may have occurred as a result of the action of police officers.

The Police Ombudsman has no power to place sanctions against a member of the PSNI, but can pass the evidence to the Public Prosecution Service (PPS) or the Chief Constable. The consequences of this can include:

- a verbal warning
- advice and guidance
- a fine
- dismissal
- a prison sentence.

Other institutions created under the Good Friday Agreement

Revised

Institutions introduced under the Good Friday Agreement

- The Civic Forum
- The North–South Ministerial Council
- The British–Irish Council/Council of The Isles
- The British Inter-Governmental Conference

Test yourself

Tested

1 Name the agreement that set up the NIHRC and the Police Ombudsman.
2 Give a reason why the NIHRC and the Police Ombudsman were established under this agreement.
3 Name five roles of the NIHRC.
4 What is the role of the Police Ombudsman?
5 What kind of things does the Police Ombudsman investigate?

Answers online

Exam practice

Tested

Explain how the Northern Ireland Human Rights Commission works to protect human rights in Northern Ireland. *(6 marks)*

Answers online

2.1: Maximising and sustaining health and well-being

Different types of health

> **What you need to know:**
> - What health means
> - The factors affecting physical, social and emotional health
> - How a person can improve their physical, social and emotional health

> **Key terms**
>
> Physical health – anything to do with the physical state of the body
>
> Social health – how a person interacts with people and society. Humans need interaction with other human beings for general well-being and good social health
>
> Emotional health – how we think, how we feel and how we control our emotions
>
> Bereavement – the death of an immediate family member or close friend

What health means

Revised ☐

Health is 'A complete state of physical, mental and social well-being and not simply the absence of disease or infirmity (illness)' (World Health Organisation).

> **Examiner tip**
>
> Learn this quote off by heart! You need to know how the different types of health can be affected (see tables below).

The factors affecting physical health

Revised ☐

Illness	Illnesses range from the common cold to life-threatening cancer and affect the way your body functions. Illness affects people in different ways.
Diet	A balanced diet provides your body with the fuel it needs in order to function. If your body is given inadequate amounts of vitamins, or too much salt, this will affect how well your body functions.
Economic factors	Those who are less well off are more likely to buy cheaper products, such as processed foods, which often contain high levels of sugar and fat. Over a period of time, this can affect physical health.
Environment	The environment in which you live can affect your physical health, for example, long-term exposure to sun can cause skin cancer, and poor air quality can lead to respiratory illnesses.
Exercise	There are many physical health benefits associated with exercise.
Genes	Poor physical health can be inherited. Some parents pass certain diseases on to their children in their genes, for example cystic fibrosis.
Parents	Parents determine what their children eat when they are young and also influence their choice of food and attitude to exercise in later life.
School	Schools can encourage exercise and healthy eating in pupils through PE and Home Economics lessons, and healthy options in canteens.
Local community	Some communities have 'green areas' and play parks for people to use. However, in communities where there is little to do, people are more likely to engage in unhealthy activities such as drug use out of boredom.

How a person can improve their physical health

Revised

- Eat a healthy balanced diet in the right proportions.
- Regularly exercise.

- Avoid smoking, drugs and excessive use of alcohol.
- Use sun protection cream on your skin.
- Have good social and emotional health.

The factors affecting social health

Revised

Housing	If you are proud of your home, you will be more likely to invite people round, so you will be more sociable. However, if you are embarrassed by where you live, you will not want people to come to your house, and so socialising could be more difficult.
School	In school you can make friends and you can build your confidence and self-esteem by having a good social life. Bullying in school can lead to people feeling threatened and insecure.
Workplace	Like school, the workplace can be a good place to make friends, interact with people and develop good communication skills. However, the workplace can also bring pressure and a heavy workload.
Computer/Internet	Social networking sites can be good for people in terms of making friends and starting a social life online. However, spending too much time in front of a computer is detrimental to social health as it does not require face-to-face social skills such as reading body language.

How a person can improve their social health

Revised

- Talk to family and peers often.
- Actively listen to people and respond to what they say.
- Develop conversational skills.
- Develop positive body language.

- Learn to accept constructive criticism.
- Treat others the way you would like to be treated.
- Meet new people.
- Try to be positive when talking to people.

The factors affecting emotional health

Revised

Loss of friendship	A loss of a friend will leave a gap in someone's life which can lead to depression or anxiety.
Bereavement	This is a life-changing event and can cause anger, denial, guilt, fear of the unknown, depression and anxiety.
Loss of job	Losing a job can lead to feelings of uselessness, inadequacy, shame and anger. It can also create money worries, which can cause stress or depression.
Moving school or house	Losing contact with friends or family can cause feelings of anxiousness, loneliness and, in extreme cases, depression and suicidal feelings.
Parental difficulties	Family conflict such as separation or divorce can be stressful, especially for young people, and can lead to stress or feelings of vulnerability and confusion.

How a person can improve their emotional health

Revised ☐

- **Start a new job** – this can give feelings of accomplishment and self-worth.
- **Form a new friendship** – this gives you someone new to talk to and share feelings with.
- **Join a club or society** – this gives you a sense of belonging and more people to socialise with.
- **Take up a new hobby or interest** – this gives you more people to talk to and makes you use your body or mind.
- **Maintain a balanced diet** – this keeps your body and brain working at an optimum level so that you are able to think clearly and deal with any issues that come your way.
- **Develop a new skill** – this can give you a sense of achievement.
- **Keep physically active** – when you exercise you release chemicals in your brain that can make you feel happy.

Examiner tip

For any of these points, your explanation can be the same, e.g. '… and this will develop your self-confidence'.

Test yourself

Tested ☐

1 Explain the term 'health'.
2 Identify three factors that can affect someone's physical health.
3 What is social health?
4 Describe someone who is socially healthy.
5 Identify three factors that can negatively affect someone's social health.

6 Explain the term 'emotional health'.
7 Identify three factors that can affect a person's emotional health.
8 Identify three ways that a person could improve their emotional health.

Answers online

Exam practice

Tested ☐

Identify and explain one way a person's emotional health may be affected by bereavement. *(2 marks)*

Answers online

Examiner tip

Often candidates get confused between emotional and social health. Make sure you read the question carefully to see what aspect of health you are expected to demonstrate your knowledge of.

Exercise

What you need to know:
- The short-term and long-term benefits of exercise
- The short-term and long-term effects of not getting enough exercise
- The factors that can affect a person's fitness

Key term

Exercise – activity that can help improve health and should be part of a healthy lifestyle

The short-term and long-term benefits of exercise

GYM

Short-term benefits:
- burns excess calories which could turn into fat if the body does not use them
- improves sleep
- increases flexibility
- increases energy levels
- increases blood flow to the brain, which improves concentration
- increases body temperature which stimulates glands, nerves, joints and the circulatory system.

Long-term benefits:
- improves body shape, muscle tone and posture
- stronger bones and muscles
- increases stamina, endurance, balance and can lead to faster reactions
- stronger immune system which helps fight against infections
- reduces the risk of certain illnesses including type 2 diabetes, coronary heart disease and certain cancers
- reduces blood pressure
- increases 'good' cholesterol and decreases 'bad' cholesterol
- helps control weight
- prevents premature ageing
- promotes healthy growth and development in children.

Examiner tip

Learn at least four short-term benefits and four long-term benefits.

The short-term and long-term effects of not getting enough exercise

Short-term effects

- Breathlessness
- Low energy levels
- A flabby body
- Being overweight
- Stiff joints and poor posture

Long-term effects

- Heart disease
- Strokes
- Diabetes
- Osteoporosis
- High blood pressure

Examiner tip

You must be able to explain why lack of exercise can lead to these consequences.

The factors that can affect a person's fitness

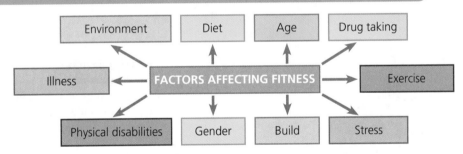

Environment · Diet · Age · Drug taking · Illness · **FACTORS AFFECTING FITNESS** · Exercise · Physical disabilities · Gender · Build · Stress

Test yourself

1 What is exercise?
2 What are three short-term benefits of exercise?
3 What are three long-term benefits of exercise?
4 Give three short-term effects of not taking exercise.

5 Give three long-term effects of not taking exercise.
6 What are three factors that can affect a person's physical fitness?

Answers online

Exam practice

Explain how exercise can improve a person's health.   *(2 marks)*

Answers online

A balanced diet

What you need to know:
- What a balanced diet means
- The benefits of eating a balanced diet
- The risks of eating an unhealthy diet
- The impact of choosing fast food, junk food and convenience food
- The arguments for and against banning the advertising of junk food
- The factors that contribute to obesity
- The risks associated with obesity
- The methods for tackling obesity

Key terms

Convenience food – food that is pre-packaged, processed and designed for quick and easy consumption, e.g. ready-made meals

Fast food – inexpensive food that is prepared and served quickly, e.g. chip shop food

Junk food – the term used to describe food that is low in nutritional value and high in calories, e.g. sweets and crisps

Obesity – the term used to describe excess body fat as calculated using the Body Mass Index (BMI)

What a balanced diet means

Revised

A balanced diet means eating the right food, consuming the correct nutrients in the right quantities and eating at regular times. A balanced diet should be made up of the five main food groups as shown in the diagram below:

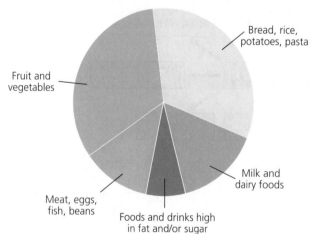

Bread, rice, potatoes, pasta

Fruit and vegetables

Milk and dairy foods

Meat, eggs, fish, beans

Foods and drinks high in fat and/or sugar

Examiner tip

You must be able to identify and explain the benefits of eating a balanced diet and the risks of eating an unhealthy diet.

A balanced diet, proportions based on the eatwell plate

The benefits of eating a balanced diet

Revised ☐

- **Physical health** – a balanced diet makes for a stronger immune system, which means your body can work to prevent and fight infections.
- **Controlling weight** – a balanced diet and correct portion sizes lead to improved control of weight and provides the body with more energy, which helps you to exercise.

- **Healthy body growth** – a balanced diet provides the body with essential nutrients, which leads to healthy growth of muscle, tissue and bone.
- **Healthy mind** – a balanced diet is beneficial to your emotional health. If you are healthy you are better able to tackle problems and make decisions and your memory should improve.

The risks of eating an unhealthy diet

Revised ☐

- **Heart disease** – high levels of fat and cholesterol clog up the arteries and can cause heart disease.
- **Poor concentration** – if your body is working hard trying to digest fatty foods, this uses up energy and reduces the ability to concentrate.
- **Lack of energy** – the body does not get the nutrients it needs from fatty foods and so cannot work at optimum level.

- **Diabetes** – fatty foods can damage the pancreas and this can lead to diabetes.
- **Obesity** – overeating means that your body is taking in more calories than it is burning and this is stored as fat.

The impact of choosing fast food, junk food and convenience food

Revised ☐

 Why people choose to eat fast food/junk food/convenience food

- taste
- low cost
- readily available
- extensive advertising
- quick or no preparation time
- can be part of a social event.

 Why people shouldn't eat fast food/junk food/convenience food

- low nutritional value
- can be addictive
- unknown food content
- fattening
- makes for an unbalanced diet
- lose the ability to cook.

The arguments for and against banning the advertising of junk food

Revised ☐

Advertising junk food should be banned because it encourages young people to eat more of it! Advertisements show the food as appealing and attractive and do not highlight that a diet of junk food is extremely unhealthy. Junk food should not be eaten because it leads to a risk of heart disease and obesity and can lead to a lack of energy and reduction in brain power. This is especially bad for children in school.

Argument for

Even if junk food advertising was banned, young people would see products in shops and have access to junk food. Eating junk food occasionally is not a bad thing, and it should be our choice whether or not we eat it.

The factors that contribute to obesity

Revised

- Genetics or inherited factors to a certain extent
- Excess fatty foods in diet
- Excess sugar in diet
- Excess carbohydrate in diet
- Little or no exercise
- Excess alcohol

The risks associated with obesity

Revised

- Coronary heart disease
- High blood pressure
- Type 2 diabetes
- Wearing away of joints
- Gallstones
- Reduced mobility
- Depression
- Premature death
- Cancer
- Breathing interruptions during sleep

The methods for tackling obesity

Revised

- Exercise
- Healthy activities
- Advice and help from a medical professional, e.g. GP
- Weight-loss organisation
- Education
- Gastric band/balloon
- Weight-loss medication
- Calorie-controlled diet
- Self-help group

Test yourself

Tested

1 What is a balanced diet?
2 Identify three reasons why it is important to eat a balanced diet.
3 Identify three risks associated with not eating a balanced diet.
4 Identify one example of the following: fast food, convenience food, junk food.
5 Explain why some people choose to eat at fast food restaurants.

6 Write a sentence explaining why some people think junk food adverts should be banned.
7 What is obesity?
8 Identify three factors that contribute to obesity.
9 Identify three risks associated with obesity.
10 Identify three things a person could do to tackle obesity.

Answers online

Exam practice

Tested

Explain two reasons for banning junk food advertisements during children's television programmes.

(4 marks)

Answers online

Drugs

What you need to know:

- How drugs can be classified
- How drugs affect the mind and body
- Why young people experiment with drugs
- The consequences of experimenting with drugs
- How those with a drug problem can be helped

Key term

Drug – any substance that affects how the body and mind work

How drugs can be classified

Revised

When we think of drugs we tend to think of illegal substances such as cannabis or cocaine but there are drugs that are legal (for example, alcohol and tobacco). Even though these drugs are legal they can still be dangerous and that is why there is legislation in place to try to stop young people from experimenting with legal drugs, for example, you have to be over 18 to buy alcohol or cigarettes.

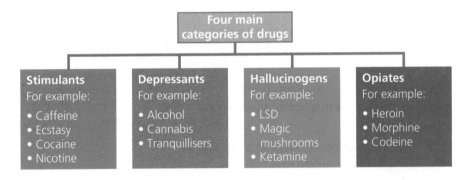

Four main categories of drugs

Stimulants
For example:
- Caffeine
- Ecstasy
- Cocaine
- Nicotine

Depressants
For example:
- Alcohol
- Cannabis
- Tranquillisers

Hallucinogens
For example:
- LSD
- Magic mushrooms
- Ketamine

Opiates
For example:
- Heroin
- Morphine
- Codeine

How drugs affect the mind and body

Revised

Drug category	How they affect the body and mind
Stimulants, e.g. tea/coffee	They speed up the central nervous system and brain activity. They make you feel euphoric, talkative and confident. This can quickly turn to agitation and aggression.
Depressants, e.g. alcohol, cannabis	They cause feelings of sleepiness and relaxation as they slow down the central nervous system and brain activity. Side effects can include clumsiness, dizziness and slurred speech.
Hallucinogens, e.g. poppers, magic mushrooms	These affect the senses and alter the drug user's perception causing hallucinations. Side effects include increased blood pressure and heart rate, flashbacks, outbursts of violence and mood swings.
Opiates, e.g. heroin	These are powerful drugs, which can be prescribed for pain relief. When abused they have the effect of blocking out feelings and making the user appear cut off from the world. Side effects include vomiting, weak muscles, reduction in heart rate and the body can become dependent on the drug.

Why young people experiment with drugs

Peer pressure: a lot of young people start taking drugs because people in their peer group are taking them and there is a pressure to fit in with everyone else.

Stress: young people can become stressed for many reasons including school, parents and **bullying**. Some may want to escape their stressful situations and may experiment with drugs to make them feel good.

Availability: many young people know where to get illegal drugs if they want them. This can make it difficult to say no. Legal drugs – for example, alcohol and nicotine – are also very accessible.

Curiosity: most young people are naturally curious. Drugs are an issue that is often talked about in school and this can lead to a desire to experiment.

WHY YOUNG PEOPLE EXPERIMENT WITH DRUGS

Pleasure: this is one of the strongest influences on young people. If a young person is under the impression that a drug makes them 'feel good', they are going to be inclined to take it.

Lifestyle: there are situations where drugs are considered to be more acceptable. For example, many young people experiment with drugs in night clubs. In some areas where there is high unemployment and low wages, drug use also increases.

Low cost: drugs can be cheaper than alcohol and the effects may last longer, so young people may see drugs as value for money.

Rebellion: young people have been told over and over by parents, school and charities how drugs are bad for them. Risk taking is a normal part of growing up and young people have a tendency to rebel during their teenage years.

The consequences of experimenting with drugs

- **School** – Drugs affect the body and mind. They can make young people feel tired and irritable and less responsible. This can therefore affect their ability to learn.
- **Family** – Drugs can change people, for example their health and their personality. This can cause a breakdown in relations in a family as parents try to help their child.
- **Siblings** – A child with a drug problem often takes centre stage in a home and this can cause a sibling to feel neglected, or the sibling may follow in the drug user's footsteps and start to take drugs too.
- **Friends** – Drug users can become withdrawn or prone to mood swings, which can be difficult for friends to handle. Friendships can also be tested if drugs users lie and refuse to accept that they have a problem.
- **Society** – Drug addiction can lead to users committing crimes in order to get money to feed their habit. There are therefore consequences for the victims of these crimes. Illness related to drug abuse costs the NHS millions each year. Absenteeism from work as a result of drug use also affects businesses and the local economy.

Examiner tip

You must be able to identify consequences and explain them. Learn at least four of these examples.

How those with a drug problem can be helped

Revised

Method	Explanation
Health professional	A GP will ask questions about the drug habit in order to ascertain the best course of action and the best type of treatment for the individual.
Counselling/ therapy	Counselling and therapy explore what led to the addiction and how to deal with those issues. This can help to prevent a relapse back into addiction.
Rehabilitation	This is where a person stays at a clinic for several weeks in order to take part in group therapy, one-to-one counselling and activities such as life skills and art therapy.
Schools	Schools should have a zero tolerance policy towards drugs and integrate drugs education into the curriculum. This can ensure students are advised to stay away from drugs.
The media	The media can be used as a tool for preventing drug use by warning teenagers and their parents of the effects of drugs.
Self-help groups	These can offer a support network to drug users. People may find it easier to give up their addiction if they have the support and help of others.
Charities	Northern Ireland's Alcohol and Drug Treatment charity – the Northern Ireland Community Addiction Service (NICAS) – offers services such as counselling and treatment on an individual basis.
The law	If someone is found in possession of drugs they can be sent to prison. Some people believe that this discourages people from using drugs.

Test yourself

Tested

1 Explain the term 'drug'.
2 Identify the four main categories of drugs.
3 For each category give one effect that it has on the mind and body.
4 Give three reasons why a young person may experiment with drugs.
5 Write three sentences explaining the consequences for a person of becoming a drug user.
6 Give three ways that drug users can be helped.

Answers online

Exam practice

Tested

Explain one consequence for a person who takes drugs.   *(2 marks)*

Answers online

Why do young people drink and smoke?

What you need to know:
- The reasons why a person may drink alcohol
- The risks and effects of alcohol
- The reasons why a person may smoke
- The risks and effects of smoking
- The debate surrounding the smoking ban

The reasons why a person may drink alcohol

Availability: alcohol is widely available. Some shops, pubs and off licences are still not as strict as they should be when it comes to asking for ID so it can be easy for a minor to get their hands on alcohol. People who are legally allowed to buy alcohol have been known to purchase alcohol for younger people.

Packaging: to date, alcohol packaging does not carry any health warnings and young people tend not to stop and think about the dangers of alcohol after purchasing. Alcohol packaging is becoming more and more attractive to young buyers. Alcopops come in a range of colours and flavours which can be very eye-catching to young people.

Peer pressure: young people may be influenced by their friends encouraging or pressurising them to drink.

Culture: young people are growing up in a 'binge-drinking' culture. Young people's views on alcohol and drunkenness are influenced more and more by culture. If they see others drinking and getting drunk around them, they may be more likely to engage in the activity themselves.

Advertising: advertising alcohol is still legal in the UK. Drink adverts can be seen on TV, billboards, posters and magazines.

Price: promotions such as happy hours or buy one get one free coupled with prices as low as 14p per unit of alcohol have led to government debates about whether alcohol being too cheap encourages young people to drink.

Home environment: approximately 40 per cent of alcoholic drinks sold are drunk at home. The home is a place where young people learn to drink. Parental attitudes to alcohol affect whether or not a young person chooses to drink when they are under eighteen.

The risks and effects of alcohol

Alcohol has the effects of a depressant. It can cause:

- clumsiness and dizziness
- violent or aggressive behaviour
- a hangover – headache, stomach ache
- slurred speech
- unpredictable behaviour
- liver disease
- death from overdose.

Examiner tip

Remember, alcohol is a depressant: it slows down the central nervous system and leads to the effects described.

The reasons why a person may smoke

Revised

Rebellion: if parents are very opposed to smoking a young person may begin smoking as a way of rebelling against their parents.

Peer pressure: young people may be influenced by their friends encouraging or pressurising them to smoke.

Media influence: seeing celebrities smoking can influence young people to begin smoking.

Enjoyment: some people genuinely enjoy the feeling of smoking and therefore continue to smoke.

Curiosity: if people see others doing something they are often curious to see what it is like themselves.

Examiner tip

The reasons why a young person smokes also helps to explain why young people ignore health warmings on cigarette packs.

The risks and effects of smoking

Revised

Smoking has the effects of a mild stimulant. It:

- is addictive
- can cause dizziness
- leaves a cigarette smell
- causes circulation problems
- causes heart disease
- causes cancer.

Examiner tip

You must be able to identify and explain the risks that smoking has on the body.

The debate surrounding the smoking ban

Revised

The smoking ban was introduced by the UK government in 2007. This made it illegal to smoke in public places and workplaces.

Advantages of the smoking ban	Disadvantages of the smoking ban
• It reduces passive smoking. • It has reduced the number of people who smoke (many people don't like the inconvenience of having to go outside). • It makes for a healthier environment in restaurants, etc. • It makes for a cleaner environment in public places and workplaces.	• It does not stop everyone smoking. • The areas outside public places are often littered with cigarettes and ashtrays. • Entrances/exits to buildings become congested, which makes it unpleasant for people walking in and out.

Test yourself

Tested

1 Give three reasons why a person may drink alcohol.
2 What are the risks of drinking alcohol?
3 Give three reasons why a person may smoke.
4 Name three risks associated with smoking.
5 When was the smoking ban introduced?
6 Give three advantages of the smoking ban.
7 Give three disadvantages of the smoking ban.

Answers online

Exam practice

Tested

Identify and explain one reason why young people ignore health warnings on cigarette packets. *(2 marks)*

Answers online

2.2: Concept of self

Personal strengths and weaknesses

What you need to know:
- What personal strengths and weaknesses mean
- The factors that can affect self-confidence, self-esteem and self-worth

Key terms

Dyscalculia – a condition whereby a person finds maths concepts difficult

Dyslexia – a condition whereby a person finds it difficult to understand written words

Self-confidence – believing in yourself and your ability to do something. With self-confidence you can cope with success and failure.

Self-esteem – how you see/feel about yourself

Self-worth – how you rate your value as a person in your relationships with others (seeing yourself as important as everyone else)

What personal strengths and weaknesses mean

Revised ☐

We all have different personal strengths and weaknesses. It is important to have an awareness of our strengths so that we can build on them and be confident about this aspect of ourselves. Strengths can include having the ability to make friends easily or having good communication skills. It is important to be aware of our weaknesses too, so that we can improve on them. Weaknesses can include being short tempered or not having good listening skills.

The factors that can affect self-confidence, self-esteem and self-worth

Revised ☐

Factor	Explanation
Success at school	Having success in any aspect at school can improve your self-confidence, as your belief in your ability to do something will be affirmed.
Peer group	Having friends that enjoy your company can be a boost to your self-worth and self-esteem as this confirms that people have a good opinion of you.
Family	If parents support and encourage their children, the children are more likely to have good self-esteem because they believe in themselves and value themselves.
Physical appearance	There is a direct link between looking good and feeling good. A person who is generally content with their appearance is more likely to have self-confidence.
Race and religion	Being part of a group can be positive. Facing discrimination, however, can affect a person's feeling of self-confidence and self-esteem.

Test yourself

Tested ☐

1 Give an explanation of self-confidence.
2 Give an explanation of self-esteem.
3 Give an explanation of self-worth.
4 Identify four factors that affect self-confidence, self-worth and self-esteem.
5 Name two common learning difficulties that young people may face.

Answers online

Tested

Exam practice

Explain how the following factors could have a positive effect on a young person's confidence:

(i) Appearance   *(2 marks)*

(ii) Relationships with friends   *(2 marks)*

Answers online

Targets and goals

What you need to know:

- What goals are
- What SMART targets are

Key terms

Goal – an ambition or something you would like to achieve in the future

Targets – series of smaller steps required to reach a goal

What goals are

Revised

A goal is an ambition or something that you would like to achieve in the future. Goals can be either short-term (e.g. 'I want to push my assessment score up by 10 per cent') or long-term (e.g. 'I want to be an engineer when I am older'). They are the culmination of a series of targets.

What SMART targets are

Revised

In order to achieve your goals it is important to set out a plan. Plans can be made up of individual targets that will help you reach your goal. You are more likely to achieve your goal if your targets are:

Specific – are the targets clear and well defined?

Measurable – can you measure whether the goal has been achieved or not?

Achievable – are the targets achievable or impossible?

Realistic – are the targets realistic or are they unlikely to be achieved?

Time bound – have your targets got deadlines?

An example of a target could be: I am going to improve my maths (specific) assessment score (measurable) by Christmas (time bound) by spending at least two hours per week studying maths (achievable and realistic).

Specific
Measurable
Achievable
Realistic
Time bound

Examiner tip

You must be able to demonstrate to the examiner that you understand (i) what a goal is and can give an example, (ii) what a SMART target is and can give an example.

Test yourself

Tested

1 What is a goal?
2 What is a target?
3 Give an example of a goal and a target.

4 Look at the target you have written. Is it SMART? Explain how it is a SMART target.

Answers online

Exam practice

Tested

Identify and explain two targets young people may set themselves to achieve good GCSE grades.

(2 marks)

Answers online

What pressures do young people face?

What you need to know:

● The common pressures faced by young people

Key terms

Peers – people of the same age

Pressure – the feeling that something or someone is pushing you towards a particular course of action

The common pressures faced by young people

Revised

Pressure to look a certain way	Pressure to look a certain way can affect self-confidence, and can lead to spending money on cosmetics, dieting, cosmetic surgery and even eating disorders.
Pressure to do well in exams	Exam results have a big effect on a young person's future, and young people can come under pressure to do well from their family, peers, teachers and themselves.
Pressure to fit in with peers	The desire to fit in with a group can often lead to a person forgetting their own morals and values and doing things they would not normally do.
Pressure to be popular	Most people want to be noticed and young people can put pressure on themselves to be popular.
Pressure to have certain possessions	Young people can put themselves under pressure to buy certain items such as the latest mobile phone or high street fashions. These can be expensive and can cause anxiety and stress for young people and their parents.
Pressure to be in a relationship	Young people can find themselves under pressure to be in a relationship, especially a sexual relationship. Young people can be apprehensive about sex or have a desire to experience it. Relationships can be negative if they are not built on respect.
Pressure to succeed in sports or other activities	Young people can place themselves under pressure to succeed, and excessive pressure to succeed can be harmful.

Test yourself

Tested

1 What is pressure?
2 Make a list of the common pressures faced by young people.

Answers online

Exam practice

Tested

Explain the effect the pressure to fit in with peers might have on a young person.

(2 marks)

Answers online

How internal and external pressures affect young people

What you need to know:
- The positive and negative impacts of pressure
- How pressure can impact on a young person

Key terms

External pressure – pressure from outside influences such as friends, the media or peers, e.g. 'All my friends are getting better scores in their mock tests than me. How am I going to keep up?'

Internal pressure – pressure that people put on themselves. It comes from within and motivates people to achieve goals and ambitions, e.g. 'I want to be successful and pass all my GCSEs by getting all Grade As and A*s.'

The positive and negative impacts of pressure

Revised

Positive impact

- Can motivate you to get things done
- Can motivate you to make a change
- Can increase your work rate
- Adds excitement to life

Negative impact

- Can lead to physical illness
- Can lead to over-reaction to small things
- Can cause disrupted sleep
- Can lead to increased use of alcohol or drugs.

Examiner tip

Learn these impacts of pressure as you can adapt them to any question that asks about the impact of peers, media, school pressure, etc.

How pressure can impact on a young person

Revised

Pressure	Positive impact	Negative impact
Media	The media can present positive role models, such as sports personalities or successful business people. This may influence a young person to behave like the people that they admire.	The media can show negative role models – people who lead unhealthy lifestyles. This may influence a young person to copy that person by taking drugs, or to admire the actions of an abusive leader.
Peer group	Friends can be a support network. For example, friends may talk each other out of risk-taking behaviour.	The desire to fit in with a peer group can sometimes cause a young person to drink alcohol or smoke.
Religion/church	Some people believe religion can instil morals and a sense of right and wrong in a young person. This can be positive if it helps to guide young people in making the right decisions.	Some people believe religion attempts to force opinions, morals and beliefs on people, and can make them feel guilty about certain activities.
School	Academic success can contribute to raising self-esteem and have a positive impact on a young person in developing their confidence.	School can put pressure on young people with excessive workload, exam-stress, bullying and pressure to succeed. This can have a negative impact on a young person's self-esteem and confidence.
Family	Parents and family can provide invaluable support and inspiration for young people, helping them to grow into independent and responsible young adults.	Parents can pressurise young people to be the best academically or at a sporting activity and this pressure can lead to stress and feelings of inadequacy.
Sporting activities	This can develop your team-working skills and if it is a physical sport can build up a person's fitness.	This can lead to pressure to succeed that could cause stress and possibly lead to aggressive behaviour.

Test yourself

1 Give an example of an internal pressure.
2 Give an example of an external pressure.
3 Explain how school can apply pressure on a young person in a positive way and a negative way.

4 Explain how family can apply positive and negative pressure on a young person.

Answers online

Exam practice

Tested

Identify and explain one way peers can have a positive affect on a young person's life.

(2 marks)

Answers online

Strategies for limiting the effects of pressure

What you need to know:
- The effects of and strategies for coping with exam pressure
- The effects of and strategies for coping with bullying
- The effects of and strategies for coping with pressure to diet
- The factors that may lead to a person developing an eating disorder
- The effects of eating disorders

Key terms

Anorexia (nervosa) – an eating disorder which occurs because a person has a distorted image of their body and which results in a loss or decline of appetite

Bulimia (nervosa) – an eating disorder where a person eats a large amount of food in a short period of time (binge) then makes themselves sick to get rid of it

The effects of and the strategies for coping with exam pressure

Revised

The effects of exam pressure

Exam pressure can cause stress and young people may feel that they cannot cope. This can lead to out of control behaviour or can have an effect on exam performance.

Coping with exam pressure

- Create a revision timetable – a timetable will help you to feel prepared and organised as the exams approach. It prevents you leaving all the studying to the last minute and then panicking before the exams.
- Take regular breaks – it is important to take breaks to exercise and eat a balanced diet in order to maintain optimum brain function and be prepared for the exams.
- Talk to someone – if you feel under pressure, parents and teachers will understand and will be able to help you deal with the pressure so that it does not reach crisis point.

The effects of and the strategies for coping with bullying

Revised ☐

The effects of bullying

Bullying damages a person's self-esteem, self-confidence and self-worth and can leave people feeling depressed, stressed, scared and intimidated.

Coping with bullying

- **It is your right to feel safe** – if you know this and are confident and secure in your environment this can help to put a bully off.
- **Tell someone** – do not keep it to yourself. A teacher, parent or carer can support you and help to deal with the bullying. Talk to someone you trust. Schools have a zero tolerance on bullying.
- **Get advice** – there are organisations that can give you advice and support and remind you that you are not alone and do not have to suffer at the hands of a bully (e.g. Bully Busters, Childline, Beatbullying, Kid power).

The effects of and the strategies to cope with pressure to diet

Revised ☐

The effects of pressure to diet

The pressure to diet can lead to a young person becoming underweight, which is very unhealthy. This pressure can cause stress and anxiety, which can lead to extreme dieting, eating disorders and self harming.

Coping with the pressure to diet

- **Eat healthily** – if you plan your meals, include all five food groups and eat five portions of fruit and vegetables daily, your body will get the nutrients it needs to work at optimum level.
- **Don't starve** – don't forget that celebrities in magazines are often airbrushed to make them look thinner or more attractive!
- **Talk to someone** – if you are worried about your eating habits, it helps to talk to someone. Know that people come in all shapes and sizes and happiness comes from within.

The factors that may lead to a person developing an eating disorder

Revised ☐

- Depression
- Stress
- Low self-esteem
- Pressure from family
- Pressure from the media.

The effects of eating disorders

Revised ☐

- Fatigue
- Constipation
- Dehydration
- Depression
- Low blood pressure
- Kidney failure
- Heart conditions.

Test yourself Tested

1 What effect could the pressure of exams have on a young person?
2 What effect could the pressure to look thin have on a young person?
3 For each of the following, give a strategy a young person could use to limit the effect of the pressure: exam pressure, bullying, dieting, parental pressure.
4 What is anorexia nervosa?
5 What is bulimia?

Answers online

Exam practice Tested

Name two dangers of a young person dieting.   *(2 marks)*

Answers online

Limiting the effects of social networking on the internet

What you need to know:
- The advantages and disadvantages of social networking
- The strategies that can be used to limit the dangers of social networking

Examiner tip

Practise an extended piece of writing on the topic 'evaluating social networking'.

Key term

Social networking – interaction with others using the internet

The advantages and disadvantages of social networking Revised

Advantages to a young person	Disadvantages to a young person
• Making new friends • Being reunited with people from the past • Building and maintaining friendships • Learning about other people's cultures • Improving social skills • Having fun • Improving IT skills • Improving literacy skills	• Risk of identity theft • People can hide their true identity online – sexual predators or stalkers have used online chat rooms to arrange meetings with victims • Cyber bullying – people can feel intimidated by what is said about them online • Prospective employers can access information you have provided online and may use this to make judgements about you • It can become addictive and important social skills may be lost

Examiner tip

You must be able to explain why a young person would feel attracted to social networking.

The strategies that can be used to limit the dangers of social networking Revised

- Never give out personal details.
- Only communicate with real friends.
- Keep your social networking site private.
- Only share videos and photos with friends.
- Never meet up with anyone you have met online.
- Never accept files or downloads from people you don't know.
- Don't get involved in online arguments.

Tested

Test yourself

1 What is social networking?
2 What are the advantages of social networking?
3 What are the disadvantages of social networking?
4 List the strategies a person could use to limit the dangers of social networking.

Answers online

Exam practice

Tested

Identify and explain two risks for a young person using internet chat rooms.

(4 marks)

Answers online

2.3: Building and maintaining healthy relationships

Relationships

What you need to know:
- What a healthy relationship is
- The factors that can affect relationships

Key term

Relationship – a connection between two people

What a healthy relationship is

Revised

In a healthy relationship, you:
- feel good about yourself
- feel safe in the other person's company
- trust the other person
- know the other person wants the best for you.

A person can have a number of different kinds of relationship:

- **Families**: this can include relationships between parents, brothers and sisters and extended family, e.g. aunts and uncles. In general, families are built on unconditional love.
- **Boyfriend/girlfriend**: this generally refers to a romantic or sexual relationship between two people.
- **Friendship**: people establish friendships throughout their lives. This kind of relationship is about mutual trust, cooperation and support. Friendships can range from short-term casual relationships or acquaintances to long-term friendships. You can also have friendships with pen pals and e-pals.

The factors that can affect relationships

Factor	Explanation
Trust	Without trust, one or both of those in the relationship could feel insecure, which can lead to arguments.
Mutual respect	Respect in a relationship means that each person values the other person for who they are.
Honesty	Not being honest can lead to feelings of guilt and can have repercussions if the lies come to light.
Communication	It is almost impossible to have a relationship without communication. Communication – verbal or nonverbal – is important for expressing and sharing opinions, values, beliefs, ideas, feelings and thoughts.
Degree of independence	People need space and time to themselves. Spending all one's spare time with one person can lead to boredom and arguments.
Compromise	Working through an argument and reaching a compromise (a bit of give-and-take) can help make a relationship stronger.
Tolerance	Being tolerant means putting up with things that annoy you. This is about respecting the fact that everyone is different.
Willingness to accept responsibility	It is important not to play the blame game and hold other people responsible if something goes wrong. Both parties need to accept responsibility to make things work.
Commitment	Being committed means making a pledge to make the relationship work through good times and bad. This means the relationship is more likely to be stable and to last.

Test yourself

1 What is a relationship?
2 What is a healthy relationship?

3 List the factors that can affect a relationship.

Answers online

Exam practice

Explain one reason why communication skills are important in a relationship.

(2 marks)

Answers online

2.4: Recognising, assessing and managing risk

What sorts of risks do young people take?

What you need to know:
- The sorts of risks young people take
- The benefits and costs of risks taken by young people
- The reasons why young people take risks
- How a young person could avoid risk-taking behaviour

The sorts of risks young people take

Revised

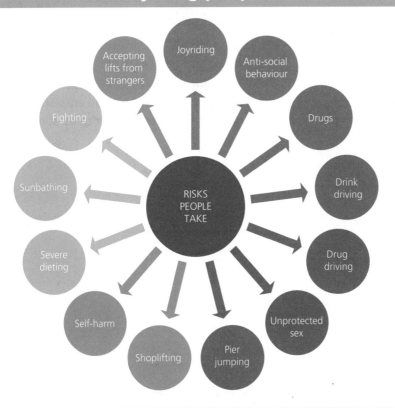

The benefits and costs of risks taken by young people

Revised

Activity	Benefits	Costs
Joyriding	Fun, thrill seeking	An innocent person could be knocked down; joyriders can be killed
Taking drugs	Escapism, coping mechanism, fun	There is the possibility of a drug overdose; it is an expensive habit and can lead to other criminal activity
Shoplifting	Having sought after items without the expense	It is illegal and you could end up with a criminal record
Sunbathing	A tan is seen as healthy	It can cause skin cancer and early ageing of the skin

The reasons why young people take risks

Revised

Being under the influence of alcohol or drugs: this can alter brain activity and cloud judgements and therefore make young people less likely to consider the consequences of their actions.

Peer pressure: a desire to impress those within the same peer group can result in young people adopting the values and beliefs of that group.

Boredom: boredom may tempt a young person into trying something that seems exciting but could be risky.

Curiosity: young people like to experience new things.

THE REASONS WHY YOUNG PEOPLE TAKE RISKS

School: some young people find school restricting and boring, and rebel in an attempt to express their individuality.

Rebelling against parents: some young people rebel against the people who had the biggest influence and control over their early lives; this is often done to prove a point or gain attention.

The media: what young people hear and read can lead them to take risks, such as trying drugs because they have heard about celebrities with drug problems.

How a young person could avoid risk-taking behaviour

- **Turn to parental/carer support** – talk to your parents/carers. They were young once and can offer advice on how to deal with tricky situations.
- **Choose friends carefully** – pick your friends based on common interests and personality compatibility and avoid people who do not accept you for who you are.
- **Evaluate the risk** – think through the behaviour and the consequences of your actions.
- **Channel energies into safer behaviour** – having a hobby or pastime means you are less likely to get bored and therefore want to do something risky.

Test yourself

1 List four different types of risk-taking behaviour.
2 For each one, give one cost and one benefit.

3 List four reasons why a young person may become involved in risk-taking behaviour.
4 List three ways a young person could avoid risk-taking behaviour.

Answers online

Exam practice

Explain one reason why a young person may put their health and safety at risk.   *(2 marks)*

Answers online

2.5: Understanding the roles and responsibilities of parenting

Parenting

What you need to know:
- The main roles of a parent
- The challenges faced by being a young parent
- The financial cost of being a parent

The main roles of a parent

Role	Explanation
To provide basic needs	By making sure the child has water, food, clothes, shelter, medical care.
To provide a safe environment	By keeping the child safe from abuse and unsafe objects.
To provide a loving environment	By spending time with, communicating with and showing affection for the child.
To provide discipline	By rewarding good behaviour and punishing bad behaviour.
To encourage and foster interests and skills	By encouraging the child to participate, acknowledging achievement and setting expectations.
To provide opportunities for social development	By organising play dates and encouraging the child to make friends.

Role	Explanation
To provide financial support	By providing money for the child's needs.
To provide support for educational development	By communicating with schools, helping with homework and celebrating achievement.
To assist in the development of morals and values	By teaching the child right from wrong and leading by example.

The challenges faced by being a young parent

Revised

Challenge	Explanation
Emotional issues	Being a parent is very emotional and young parents are more likely to face postnatal depression, stress and fear of failure.
Social stigma	Some people look down on young parents and this can affect young parents' self-esteem and self-confidence.
Social life	Young parents will not be able to interact with their friends as much as other people their age and this can affect their social and emotional health.
Financial issues	Raising a child is expensive. Young parents may have to rely on family, friends and benefits and this can lead to stress and be emotionally challenging.
Career prospects	Staying in full-time education can be difficult for young parents and so they may need to forsake long-term career plans.
School	The education of young parents is dramatically affected and they may not reach their full potential or goals.
Health	Teenage mothers are more likely to suffer premature or prolonged labour. Being a parent is also physically demanding which can lead to depression.
Absence of a father	Teenage relationships face considerable challenges because people tend to change as they get older. Therefore, some teenage mothers have to bring up a child without the help of a father, which is particularly stressful as all the responsibility of parenting rests on one person.

The financial cost of being a parent

Revised

Babies are very expensive, as indicated by this list of essentials for a newborn baby:

- Nappies
- Bottles
- Blankets
- Cot/Moses basket
- Pram
- Clothes – hats, babygros
- Baby monitor
- Baby wipes/cotton wool.

Before a baby is born, the essential items will need to be bought, which could cost around £1,600. There is also more pressure on parents to buy fashionable items – some prams cost £700 or more. The average family can spend nearly £9,500 on a baby in its first year. The cost of bringing up a child from birth to 18 years can be well over £150,000.

Examiner tip

If a question asks you to identify and explain challenges faced by parents, don't focus only on the financial challenges. Learn at least three other types of challenge that parents face.

Test yourself

Tested

1 List four of the roles of being a parent.
2 List four ways a parent can fulfil these roles.
3 List four of the challenges faced by being a young parent.
4 Write a sentence explaining why having a baby can be a financial challenge to a young person.

Answers online

Exam practice

Tested

Explain the main responsibilities when becoming a parent.　　*(6 marks)*

Answers online

2.6: Developing competence as discerning consumers

Key terms relating to money

What you need to know:
- The advantages of budgeting
- The consequences of not sticking to a budget
- Strategies to help a person stick to a budget

Key terms

APR (Annual Percentage Rate) – the interest a borrower is charged over one year on any loans or credit cards. The lower the APR, the better for the borrower

Budget – a tool to manage money coming in (income) and money spent (expenditure)

Credit card – a commonly accepted form of payment, which can also be used to withdraw cash. Credit card companies give people credit up to a certain limit and send out monthly bills with a minimum amount to be repaid. The money spent has to be paid back with interest over time and so the quicker the debt is paid off, the less money is paid to the credit card company

Debit card – used to take out (debit) the value of goods or services from the bank account linked to the card. Going overdrawn with a debit card can incur bank charges

Debt – the amount of money that one person owes to other people or organisations

Loan shark – a person that offers unsecured loans at very high interest rates to individuals, sometimes backed by blackmail or violence. An unsecured loan allows you to borrow money without having to provide security against it, such as your house or car

The advantages of budgeting

Revised

- Makes it easier to keep track of and control spending
- Shows where you are spending too much
- Can relieve money-related stress
- Can help with debt management
- Can help free up and save money
- Can help with investing money
- Can help prepare for emergencies.

The consequences of not sticking to a budget

Revised

- You may fall into debt
- You may not be able to reach your goals
- You may not be able to pay for essential items
- You will not be able to save money
- You will not be able to keep track of your money and this can cause stress.

Strategies to help a person stick to a budget

Revised

- **Stay motivated** – keep your goals in mind. This will help to keep you motivated to stick to your budget.
- **Keep your budget up to date** – regularly check and update the budget. This will help you keep focused on your goals.
- **Treat yourself** – factor in money for fun. This will help to keep you motivated.

- **Be self-disciplined** – recognise that it takes will power to change your spending habits.
- **Consider quality v. price** – research items to see if you can save money elsewhere as cheaper items can sometimes be of inferior quality.
- **Be realistic** – create a budget that reflects what you can afford.

Test yourself

Tested

1 What is a credit card?
2 What is a debit card?
3 What is APR?
4 What is a loan shark?
5 What is a budget?
6 Give three reasons why it is good to budget.
7 Give two consequences of not budgeting.

Answers online

Exam practice

Tested

Explain one reason why it is beneficial to have a household budget.   *(2 marks)*

Answers online

Consumer choices

What you need to know:
- The advantages and disadvantages of buying for quality or for price
- The advantages and disadvantages of buying with cash or with credit
- The advantages and disadvantages of buying new or second-hand
- The difference between a want and a need
- The advantages and disadvantages of buying and renting

The advantages and disadvantages of buying for quality or for price

Revised

Quality	
Advantage	**Disadvantage**
A product of better quality will last longer and therefore save money in the longer term	You cannot be guaranteed that a product which is more expensive is better quality because it might just be over-priced
	All products, regardless of quality, can have faults

Price	
Advantage	**Disadvantage**
A cheaper product may be good value for money	It may need to be replaced more quickly
A cheaper product may be all that can be afforded	It may not provide the same service as a more expensive product

The advantages and disadvantages of buying with cash or with credit

Revised

Cash		Credit	
Advantages	**Disadvantages**	**Advantages**	**Disadvantages**
Can make budgeting easier	Less convenient, you have to search for an ATM	More convenient than cash	Can lead to overspending if not managed carefully
Handing over cash tends to lead to less spending	If you lose your wallet, cash might not be returned	Credit can be easily obtained	Some companies charge a monthly fee
Less likely to be subject to identity fraud	Carrying a large amount of cash can make you a target for criminals	Can track spending online	Can lead to debt
		Buyer protection means you are less vulnerable to online scams	Can be expensive if interest rates are high
		Credit cards can be replaced if lost or stolen	Credit cards can be an easy target for criminals

The advantages and disadvantages of buying new or second-hand

Revised

New	
Advantages	**Disadvantages**
Buying new can give a great sense of satisfaction and pride as no one else has owned it first	New is more expensive than second-hand which some people may not be able to afford
A new item will come with a warranty or guarantee	New does not guarantee that a product will last longer or not be faulty
Second-hand	
Advantages	**Disadvantages**
This may be all that can be afforded	It will not have a guarantee
It can be good value for money	It may need repairs or need to be replaced more quickly

The difference between a want and a need

Revised

Spending money on what you actually need should be a priority before spending money on things you want.

- **Want** – a luxury item that you do not need for survival, e.g. chocolate cake, car, internet, XBOX, mobile phone

- **Need** – an essential item for survival, e.g. food, clothing, home, electricity or gas, furniture

The advantages and disadvantages of buying and renting

Advantages

- Greater sense of independence and increased self-esteem.
- You own the property so can make improvements or build extensions.
- It is possible to rent out rooms or your driveway to generate extra income.
- You can turn your house into a business – for example, a B&B.
- Any improvements made are likely to increase the value of the property.
- Selling the house for more than the purchase price can lead to big profits.
- Home owners tend to have a higher social standing.

Disadvantages

- Many people don't have the capital (money) to buy a house and so need to take out a mortgage.
- Mortgage repayment rates can vary and generally have high interest rates so you end up paying a lot more than you borrowed.
- Failing to keep up with mortgage repayments can mean losing your house.
- The value of the house can decrease meaning you would lose money if it was resold. In this case you may be repaying a mortgage for more than the value of the property (this is referred to as 'negative equity').

Advantages and disadvantages of buying a property

Advantages

- Renting is generally cheaper than paying off a mortgage and the rent doesn't fluctuate.
- Renting is usually short-term, with lease periods of a year or less.
- Landlords are responsible for the upkeep of the property, including plumbing, heating, electrical wiring and sometimes
- The provision of electrical goods such as fridges and ovens if specified in the lease.

Disadvantages

- You may have to move and seek alternative accommodation when the lease expires.
- You may have to share accommodation with strangers or people you dislike.
- You might not have any say over decoration or renovations.
- You won't own the house and so many people see renting as throwing money away.

Advantages and disadvantages of renting accommodation

Test yourself

1. Give two advantages of buying a quality product.
2. Give two disadvantages of buying a cheaper product.
3. Give two advantages of using cash.
4. Give two disadvantages of using cash.
5. Give two advantages of using credit.
6. Give two disadvantages of using credit.
7. Give an advantage of buying new.
8. Give a disadvantage of buying second-hand.
9. What is a want? Give an example.
10. What is a need? Give an example.
11. Give two advantages and disadvantages of buying property.
12. Give two advantages and disadvantages of renting.

Answers online

Exam practice

Evaluate the influence and use of credit cards in today's society. *(10 marks)*

Answers online

Debt

What you need to know:
- The reasons why a person may fall into debt
- The consequences of falling into debt
- The strategies for coping with debt and becoming debt free

The reasons why a person may fall into debt
Revised

Poor health: if you are not able to work you won't be able to earn money and may have medical/care bills to pay.

Poor budgeting: spending more than you earn may mean going into debt in order to pay bills.

Loss of a job: losing a job will affect household income meaning difficulty in paying bills or meeting repayments.

Unexpected spending: unforeseen expenditures – for example, a car repair – may take a person by surprise and they may need to borrow money to pay the bill.

HOW PEOPLE FALL INTO DEBT

Increase in the size of a family: an unexpected pregnancy or an elderly/sick relative coming to live with a family will increase the amount of money that has to be spent within the household. This could mean a family may have to borrow money to cope with the added pressure.

Gambling addiction: a person who is addicted to gambling may be unable to stop despite the negative consequences and can run up large debts.

Drug addiction: drug addicts will beg, borrow or steal to feed their drug habit which can lead to debt.

The consequences of falling into debt
Revised

- **Legal** – you could be taken to court for non-payment and end up being declared bankrupt.
- **Loss of property** – you could lose your home, car or other possessions if you fail to keep up with repayments.
- **Emotional health** – the stress and worry can leave you emotionally unwell or suffering from depression and anxiety.
- **Social stigma** – people in debt are often looked down upon. Those in debt may fear the reaction of their family, which can add stress.
- **Crime** – if a person feels that they cannot pay off their debt they may look at illegal options.
- **Spiral into further debt** – some people borrow money to pay off debt. This is referred to as the debt cycle.

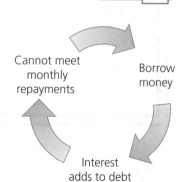

The debt cycle

The strategies for coping with debt and becoming debt free

Coping strategy	Explanation
Seek advice	Consumer Credit Counselling Service (CCCS) and Citizens Advice Bureau (CAB) provide free impartial advice.
Talk to family and friends	Family and friends may be able to offer help, support and advice on possible strategies.
Evaluate your budget	Re-examine or create a personal budget to reduce expenditure.
Talk to the creditor	The creditor may revise your payment plan to help you meet payments.
Consolidate loans	Bringing all your loans together means you have to deal with only one company.
Shop around	Try to move loans to organisations with lower interest rates.
Bankruptcy	Bankruptcy means you will not have to pay your debts but it may make it difficult to borrow money in the future.

Test yourself

1 Give three reasons why a person may end up in debt.
2 Give three consequences for a person who ends up falling into debt.

3 Give three actions a person in debt could take to help become debt free.

Answers online

Exam practice

Explain two reasons why people may end up in debt.   *(2 marks)*

Answers online

3.1: The impact of globalisation on employment

Globalisation

What you need to know:
- Why a business would go global
- What imports and exports mean
- The impact of globalisation on Northern Ireland

Key terms

Consumer – an individual who buys goods or services for personal use

Trading – the business of buying and selling

Imports – goods or services which are brought into a country from another country

Exports – goods or services that are sold to another country

Global – involving the entire earth; worldwide

Globalisation – the movement of goods, people and ideas around the world

Global economy – the system of industry and trade around the world that has developed as a result of globalisation

Why a business would go global

Revised ☐

The reasons for a business going global can be summed up by 3Cs: cost, climate and competition.

Cost

It is cheaper to produce some goods in other countries rather than in Northern Ireland, due to factors such as a cheaper workforce, cheaper raw materials or cheaper utilities.

- **Benefit to consumer** – products sold in shops may be cheaper.

- **Benefit to business** – possibly more profit if the cost of producing the goods is lowered (less overheads). With cheaper products, businesses can be more competitive and attract more customers thus resulting in increased profit.

Climate

Some countries can produce goods that cannot be produced in Northern Ireland, for example coffee, so the goods are imported for sale here. We import fruit and vegetables from other countries where they can be grown all year round.

- **Benefit to consumer** – greater choice of goods.

- **Benefit to business** – a greater choice of goods can attract more customers and increase profit.

Competition

There may be an opportunity to sell products in other countries in competition with other global or local businesses. The goods or services a business could sell may not be on offer in another country, or they may be able to provide higher quality or cheaper goods or services.

- **Benefit to consumer** – more choice and better quality products and services.

- **Benefit to business** – selling products in other countries could result in increased profit for the business and more job opportunities.

What imports and exports mean

Imports are goods or services that are brought into a country from another country. Exports are goods or services that are sold to another country. In the UK we import from and export to many different countries.

Top five UK exports in 2009	Top five UK imports in 2009
Medicines	Cars
Petrol	Petrol
Cars	Aerospace
Other oils	Telecoms
Engines/motors	Medicines

This exchange of goods provides employment.

> **Examiner tip**
>
> Make sure you read the exam question carefully. You may be asked to discuss the implications of a global economy for:
>
> - the business/employer
> - the employee
> - the consumer
> - Northern Ireland.

The impact of globalisation on Northern Ireland

Benefits of globalisation to a business

- Globalisation gives a business a larger market and so this could lead to increased trade
- Export opportunities in a global market, which can lead to increased profit

- The opportunity to learn more efficient business methods through the sharing of ideas with other countries in the global market.

Disadvantages of globalisation to a business

- More competition for local businesses. In a global market, business from other countries can compete for a share in the local market
- Closure of businesses due to the increased competition of being in a global market
- Fluctuation in money markets – if a business is importing into the UK the price of the good will depend on the strength of the pound against the currency of the other country, e.g. if Tesco buys Belgian chocolates at one euro a unit, it will cost much more if one euro is worth 90p than if one euro is worth 70p

- Money will be needed for retraining of staff to work in a global market, e.g. to deal with the skills needed to break into foreign markets
- Language barriers – it can be difficult to communicate in a market (particularly with customers) where a different language is spoken
- Transport arrangements can be expensive and take time to organise, which may mean that the business may lose money in the short term.

Benefits of globalisation to an employee

- Opportunity for employees to gain new skills or promotion as the business expands and new job roles become available.

Disadvantages of globalisation to an employee

- Redundancies due to under-pricing from foreign businesses

- Pressure may be placed on employees to travel to other countries and to remain there to establish a business.

Benefits of globalisation to a consumer

- Variety of products and services and a larger range of service or goods providers

- Increased competition can lead to better value.

Benefits of globalisation to Northern Ireland

- Opportunity to trade on an equal basis with countries all over the world
- Attracting investment in jobs/communities in Northern Ireland
- Tourism into Northern Ireland
- Civic pride as the country is able to compete in a global market

- Educational, community and business links, e.g. town twinning (the partnering of cities for sharing of ideas, innovation and culture)
- Building relationships with countries around the world.

Test yourself

Tested

1 Explain the term 'globalisation'.
2 Explain the term 'import'.
3 Give one example of goods imported to the UK.

4 Give one example of goods exported from the UK.
5 List five benefits of trading globally.
6 List five disadvantages of trading globally.

Answers online

Exam practice

Tested

Evaluate the impact of a global economy on Northern Ireland.   (10 marks)

Answers online

The impact of changing employment patterns on Northern Ireland

What you need to know:
- What employment patterns mean
- How employment patterns have changed
- Why employment patterns have changed
- Why teamwork is an important skill in the workplace

> **Key terms**
>
> **Primary sector** – the sector of industry that harvests or extracts raw materials or products from the earth
>
> **Secondary sector** – the manufacturing part of industry
>
> **Tertiary sector** – the service sector of industry
>
> **Teamwork** – work performed by a team of people working towards a common goal
>
> **Teleworking** – working at home while communicating with the employer by phone, fax or computer

What employment patterns mean

Revised ☐

Employment patterns refer to the types of jobs we do, who employs us and how many of us are employed at a given time.

Type of job

Primary sector
- Farming
- Fishing
- Mining
- Oil drilling
- Forestry

Secondary sector
- Manufacturing
- Construction

Tertiary sector
- Services: business/public

Type of employment

- **Permanent** (full time/part time) – an employee with paid leave entitlements and a work contract of unlimited duration
- **Temporary** (full time/part time) – an employee with a fixed-term contract
- **Seasonal** – a worker who finds employment in certain seasons, e.g. Christmas
- **Freelance** – a person who sells services to employers without a long-term commitment to any of them
- **Teleworking** – working from home

Type of employer

- **Self-employed** – working for yourself
- **Public sector** – working for the government
- **Private sector** – working for a private business

How employment patterns have changed

Revised ☐

Over the last 30 years, many changes have occurred in employment patterns within the UK. These include:

- more women in work
- growth in the number employed in the public sector (this is changing, as the government aims to reduce the number of workers in the public sector)
- growth in the service industries such as banking, IT and tourism
- decline in manufacturing industries such as shipbuilding
- changing employee and consumer demands.

Why employment patterns have changed

Revised

- **Advances in technology** – technology is constantly changing and these changes bring about a change in the jobs offered and skills required by employers. The introduction of machinery and computerisation in many industries has resulted in a reduction in staff, and trends are now based in computerisation.
- **Availability of appropriately skilled workers** – because of developments in technology and in a global market, employees need to learn new skills for the growing tertiary (services) sector.
- **Cost of the labour force** – as a result of globalisation, many companies based in Northern Ireland have decided to have their goods produced abroad because of the cheaper workforce. People employed in factories in Northern Ireland therefore face losing their jobs and having to retrain to have the employability and technological skills that are most sought after.

Examiner tip

You must be able to identify and explain reasons why employment patterns are changing.

Why teamwork is an important skill in the workplace

Revised

Teamwork is an important skill in the workplace because it:

- enables the sharing of ideas and creativity
- makes for healthy competition amongst staff
- can lead to a more equal distribution of work
- can lead to increased production
- gives members of the team a sense of responsibility
- brings job satisfaction
- can mean lower stress levels.

Examiner tip

You must be able to explain why these points are important for employees and employers. Remember to fully explain your answers in the exam using connecting words (see page 3).

The benefits of teleworking

- It reduces the need for office space.
- It allows employees to have flexible working hours to suit their needs.

Test yourself

Tested

1 List three ways in which employment patterns have changed.

2 List three reasons why employment patterns have changed.

Answers online

Exam practice

Tested

Explain one benefit to an employee of teleworking. *(2 marks)*

Answers online

The impact of immigration and emigration on Northern Ireland

What you need to know:
- The reasons why people migrate
- The reasons for immigration to Northern Ireland
- The advantages and disadvantages of immigration into Northern Ireland
- Why people leave Northern Ireland
- The advantages and disadvantages of emigration from Northern Ireland

Key terms

Migration – the process of people moving between countries

Immigrants – people who move into another country

Immigration – the process of coming to live in a foreign country

Emigrants – people who have left their own country to go elsewhere

Emigration – the movement of people to another country

Examiner tip

Ensure you give an explanation if a question asks you about the reasons why people migrate.

The reasons why people migrate

Revised

- **Employment** – other countries may have more job opportunities than the home country
- **Moving to a place where your skills are required** – some countries have a skills shortage and if you have the skill that is sought after you may be offered an incentive to go to that country and work
- **Better pay and conditions** – this can be the case if the country is more developed and more modern
- **Better standard of living** – if there are more activities to participate in or more amenities in that country due to climate
- **To avoid war** – many people do not want to remain in a country that is being ravaged by war

- **To avoid persecution** – in countries where human rights are abused
- **For medical treatment** – if the country has superior medical services
- **To avoid racism** – in some countries certain people face violence or live in fear of their lives because of their race
- **Retirement** – to go and live in a place with a better climate and standard of living
- **Reuniting families** – if they have been separated for many years and decide to come back together
- **To return to their country of birth** – to see family again or just experience their place of birth.

The reasons for immigration to Northern Ireland

Revised

For a number of reasons there has been a significant growth in immigration into Northern Ireland from countries outside the United Kingdom since 2004, as shown overleaf.

- Northern Ireland offers higher salaries than some other countries.
- UK-based employment agencies may have travelled to an immigrant's country and offered work.

- Northern Ireland has a better standard of living in terms of housing, education and health care than some other countries.

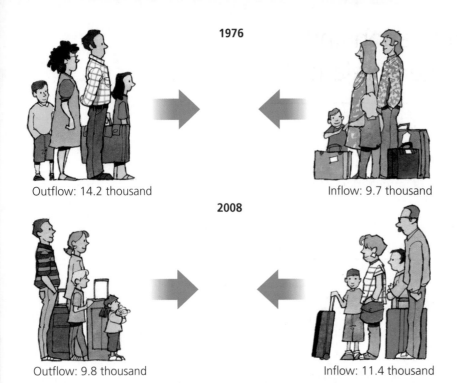

1976

Outflow: 14.2 thousand

Inflow: 9.7 thousand

2008

Outflow: 9.8 thousand

Inflow: 11.4 thousand

Diagram showing the outflow and inflow of people to and from Northern Ireland in 1976 and 2008. It shows that in the 1970s more people left Northern Ireland than came to live there. In 2008 the situation was reversed. This may be because there is more political stability now than there was in the 1970s.

Immigration into Northern Ireland has now started to level off due to a downturn in the economy, particularly in the secondary sector.

The advantages and disadvantages of immigration into Northern Ireland

Revised

Advantages to immigrants	Disadvantages to immigrants
Better pay	Racism
Better life	Poorly paid work
Better education system	Prejudice
Better health service and benefit system	Poor housing conditions
Most people are welcoming	Language barrier
	Exclusion from society
Advantages to Northern Ireland	**Disadvantages to Northern Ireland**
More choice of employees for employers	More competition for job vacancies
Migrant workers can fill job vacancies that other workers 'do not want'	Migrant workers may mask skills gaps
Migrant workers can bring new ways or different approaches to completing tasks or solving problems	Migrants may not stay in Northern Ireland – taking their skills and expertise with them
Bring cultural diversity to Northern Ireland – language, food, music	Migrant workers may not spend their wages here and send money back to their home country, which will not help Northern Ireland's economy

Examiner tip

Make sure you can identify and explain the advantages or disadvantages to the immigrant and to the country. Always read the questions carefully to ensure you answer from the correct perspective.

Why people leave Northern Ireland

- Unhappy with the post-conflict situation
- A warmer, drier climate
- Attracted to a different culture
- Opportunities for children – education, sport
- Better career opportunities – promotion, need for skills

- Change of lifestyle and type of living – for example, outdoor activities, beach lifestyle, large city environment
- Study in a different location and decide to stay there.

The advantages and disadvantages of emigration from Northern Ireland

Advantages to emigrants/NI	Disadvantages to Northern Ireland
The people leaving may gain a better standard of living	Brain drain – loss of highly skilled professionals
Better job opportunities and chances of promotion	Loss of highly skilled professionals can lead to jobs not being filled
Emigration is not permanent and people who have emigrated may return, bringing back their experience and expertise to be put to good use and shared	The movement of one individual can cause a chain reaction in a family and filter out into a community

Test yourself

1 Give an explanation of each of the following terms:
   a) migration   b) immigration   c) emigration.
2 List three reasons why someone would immigrate to Northern Ireland.
3 List three reasons why someone would emigrate from Northern Ireland.

Answers online

Exam practice

Explain the advantages of immigration for Northern Ireland.   *(6 marks)*

Answers online

The impact of the growth of new technologies on Northern Ireland

What you need to know:
- The different types of new technology that are available
- The ways in which new technology has influenced our lifestyles
- The advantages and disadvantages of new technologies
- How the growth of new technology has impacted on businesses
- How the growth of new technology has impacted on jobs

The different types of new technology that are available

Revised

- Home computers
- Compact discs
- World Wide Web
- MP3 players (e.g. iPod)
- Smart phones (e.g. iPhone)
- Tablet computers (e.g. iPad).

The ways in which new technology has influenced our lifestyles

Revised

The ability to use the computer at home and access the World Wide Web has influenced our lifestyles. We can now shop online, compare prices and communicate with each other without leaving our homes. These facilities have been enhanced further by smartphones, which mean that we can now use the World Wide Web on the move.

The advantages and disadvantages of new technologies

Revised

Advantages	Disadvantages
• Ease of access to information	• Information overload
• Ease of access to price comparisons	• Price comparison can be time consuming and often does not include transport/delivery costs
• Ease of communication	• Dangerous as people can be subject to abuse or fraud
• Home entertainment	
• Ability to work from home	

How the growth of new technology has had an impact on businesses

Revised

If a business wants to remain competitive in the global market then it must seek out and use the latest technologies in order to keep one step ahead of the competition.

Advantages

Some tasks become easier and more manageable if they are computerised. This can mean fewer employees are needed, which saves the business money.

Disadvantages

Staff need a different skills set and it may be difficult to find the staff with these skills, particularly if new technology continues to grow at the rate it has. Also, transferring to a computerised system can be expensive, which may mean that the company experiences a loss initially.

How the growth of new technology has had an impact on jobs

Revised

Some jobs that were common are no longer in existence because of the growth of new technologies.

Jobs in decline

- **Travel agents** – people now use the internet to research and book holidays
- **Typists** – people now complete these activities themselves using a computer
- **Factory jobs** – computers and robots can now perform some of these tasks more efficiently.

Test yourself

1 List three new technologies that have come into existence in the past 20 years.
2 Choose one new technology and explain how it has had an impact on people's lifestyles.

3 What is an advantage of the growth of new technologies?
4 What is a disadvantage of the growth of new technologies?
5 What impact has the growth of new technologies had on jobs?

Answers online

Exam practice

Explain how technology has resulted in changes in employment patterns over the past number of years. *(6 marks)*

Answers online

3.2: Recruitment and selection practices for employment

Lifelong learning

What you need to know:
- What lifelong learning means
- The reasons why a person may pursue lifelong learning
- The advantages and disadvantages of lifelong learning
- What training means
- The benefits of training
- The advantages and disadvantages of on the job and off the job training
- The organisations that can help with retraining and the development of new skills

Key terms

Lifelong learning – the process of continuing to develop skills, knowledge and expertise throughout life

Induction – the process of introducing a new employee to the workings of a new business. It will usually include information about health and safety and an understanding of the history and goals of the business

On the job training – training that is conducted within the workplace

Off the job training – training that is conducted outside the workplace

What lifelong learning means

Lifelong learning is the idea that our education and our learning of new skills do not end when we leave school or university. Therefore, we should continue to learn throughout our career during staff training and development.

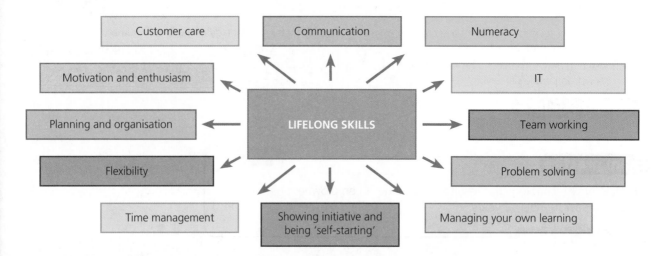

The reasons why a person may pursue lifelong learning

- As the world of work changes it is important to develop existing skills and acquire new skills.
- There is a need for more qualifications in order to meet the demands of a changing society.
- More qualifications may lead to promotion and consequently a better salary.
- Developing new skills can lead to increased motivation and greater job satisfaction.
- Gaining qualifications/skills can raise self-esteem.

Examiner tip

You must be able to explain the reasons why a person may pursue lifelong learning. (Remember to use your connecting words, see page 3.)

The advantages and disadvantages of lifelong learning

Advantages	Disadvantages
• You are constantly evolving and learning new skills and thus making yourself more employable.	• It can be expensive.
• You can improve your chance of promotion.	• It can be time consuming – you may spend more time learning new skills than on your work.
• You may be able to command a better salary.	• You may miss out on family time and social engagements.
• You are able to provide a better service for your customer/business.	• You may feel disappointed if new skills or qualifications do not lead to promotion.
• You may improve your self-esteem and sense of loyalty to the job.	• It can leave you feeling tired and stressed.
• It allows people to meet the needs of an ever changing employment market.	• You could be seen as overqualified for some jobs.

What training means

Training involves learning a new skill or piece of knowledge, usually in order to perform a job or to improve current working practices. The benefits of training are that you can become an expert in your field and provide a high quality professional service. This may result in the business being able to charge a premium for these services. Training leads to a skilled workforce and this means that work will be carried out more efficiently and according to all health and safety laws.

An employee may be given training:

- as part of their induction
- because of a change in procedures
- in order to make the business more competitive (more highly skilled and more able to provide efficient and quality services).

Examiner tip

Practise answering this as an extended piece of writing: 'evaluating the impact of lifelong learning'.

The benefits of training

Benefits of training for the business/employer

- Helps the business cope with changes in technology.
- Employees will have up to date knowledge, which will ultimately benefit the organisation.
- Creates a more efficient workforce as workers may be more motivated.
- Employees can gain different skills, which means that their work can become more effective and ultimately they can undertake different tasks.
- Fewer accidents as employees know how to operate machinery correctly (which reduces staff absenteeism).
- Employees should produce a better quality of products/services.
- Less supervision of workers needed if workers know how to do tasks, are motivated and can operate machinery and equipment correctly.

Benefits of training for employees

- Training updates employees' skills and helps them cope with changes in technology.
- Employees who have kept their skills up to date have better opportunities for promotion.
- Training motivates employees as it helps them to be good at their jobs and may help them earn more.

The advantages and disadvantages of on the job and off the job training

On the job training

Advantages	Disadvantages
• Cheaper to carry out than off the job training.	• The trainer may find it difficult to deliver effective training to colleagues.
• Employees who are new to a job role become productive more quickly.	• There may be distractions in the workplace, which might lessen the effectiveness of the training.
• Training is very relevant and practical, dealing with day to day requirements of the job.	• The training may not be certified and it may not be deemed as a qualification – there is no evidence on paper.
• Employees are not taken away from jobs so they can still be productive.	• Employees may pick up bad habits from the person who is training them as they are not a professional trainer.
• Employees continue to earn money while they learn new skills.	• If employees are only trained in one area this may mean that they will require further training at a later date if they move into a different area.

Off the job training

Advantages	Disadvantages
• Employees learn from specialists in that area of work who can provide more in-depth understanding.	• Can be expensive.
• Employees respond better when taken away from the pressures of the working environment.	• May be time consuming and employees are not getting hands on experience in the workplace.
• Employees may be able to gain qualifications or certificates.	• Time away from the workplace means work is not getting done and this could cost the business in profit.
• Trainers can deal more easily with groups of employees at the same time.	• It can be ineffective and unconnected to the employees' actual roles in work.
• The training can be more focused on the needs and levels of expertise of the employees.	• The trainers may not be fully aware of the conditions under which the employees work.

The organisations that can help with retraining and the development of new skills

Organisation	How it can help
learndirect	Offers a range of business and ICT courses that you can complete online and work on at your own pace.
Job Centres	Give guidance and advice and organise training courses if you need to retrain.
Institutes of Further and Higher Education	Provide a range of vocational courses, some of which are targeted towards specific businesses.
The Careers Service of Northern Ireland	Provides a range of support for people who are in school, unemployed or wanting to change careers. Provides information on the labour market, training and qualifications available.
Educational Guidance Service for Adults (EGSA)	Provides a free service to adult learners, or anyone interested in improving access to learning for adults. Aims to connect adults with learning.

Test yourself

1 What is the meaning of lifelong learning?
2 What are the reasons why someone would pursue lifelong learning?
3 What are the advantages of lifelong learning?
4 What are the disadvantages of lifelong learning?
5 List the advantages for an employee of receiving training.

6 List the disadvantages for an employer of providing training.
7 What is the meaning of:
  a) on the job training   b) off the job training?
8 For each type of training above, list the advantages of this type of training.
9 What sources of further learning are available to adults?

Answers online

Exam practice ———————————————— Tested

Identify and explain two benefits to an employer of training staff. *(4 marks)*

Answers online ——

How has the 'credit crunch' affected employment?

What you need to know:
- What the credit crunch is and why it happened
- The consequences of the credit crunch

What the credit crunch is and why it happened — Revised

The credit crunch is the name used to describe when banks and other financial institutions such as credit unions and building societies decided to tighten up on the amount of money they would lend. The result of this was that it became more difficult for businesses and people to get credit.

The credit crunch happened because financial institutions were not able to lend money because too much money had been borrowed around the world and it wasn't being paid back. Therefore the banks stopped lending so much – they 'crunched' the credit.

Examiner tip

You must be able to identify and explain reasons for the credit crunch and consequences of the credit crunch.

The consequences of the credit crunch — Revised

- House prices plummeted leaving some home owners with negative equity (a mortgage that is worth more than the house).
- A lot of small businesses had to close.
- Public spending has been cut.
- There have been many job losses, many through redundancies.
- People have been affected by the collapse of companies such as Farepak and travel companies.

Jobs affected by the credit crunch	How and why the credit crunch affected those jobs
Construction: developers, builders, contractors, suppliers, estate agents	The demand for new housing fell dramatically as people wanting new homes could no longer get mortgages. This meant a drop in the number of new homes being built.
Retail	People no longer had access to as much credit as they did previously. Some people ended up in negative equity and were therefore more wary about spending money on luxury goods. Many retail giants suffered as a result of this, for example Woolworths.
Hospitality: bars, clubs restaurants	People have less disposable income and so go out to bars, restaurants and clubs less often.
Public sector	The government announced a decrease in public spending, which meant decreasing the wage bill in the public sector, so there were fewer jobs available in this sector.

The table above is a summary of the main sectors affected by the credit crunch but many other people have also been affected, including the elderly, people who have saved their money in banks and people on benefits.

Examiner tip

You must be able to explain why certain jobs have been affected by the credit crunch.

Test yourself

Tested ☐

1 Why did the credit crunch happen?
2 What jobs were affected by the credit crunch?

Answers online

Exam practice

Tested ☐

Identify and explain a job sector that has been affected by the credit crunch. *(2 marks)*

Answers online

The competencies and personal qualities valued by employers

What you need to know:

- The competencies and personal qualities that are valued by employers
- Why employers value these skills and qualities
- How to cope with working part time and studying
- The advantages and disadvantages of working part time and studying

The competencies and personal qualities that are valued by employers

Revised ☐

Literacy skills: the ability to communicate, through talking and listening, reading and writing

Commitment: the ability to stick with a situation or person even when things are difficult

ICT skills: the ability to use technology such as email and desktop publishing to communicate and distribute information

Numeracy skills: the ability to manipulate numbers and figures and decode diagrams and graphs

Loyalty: the ability to believe in and stick up for something or someone when it is being attacked or questioned

Flexibility: the ability to adapt skills, time and resources to make sure they are being utilised in the best possible way in any given circumstances

These skills and qualities are valued by employers for a number of reasons, for example:

- loyalty means that the employee will always act in the best interests of the business (e.g. they might promote the business amongst family and friends and are less likely to steal from the business)
- ICT skills mean that employees can perform basic tasks such as email and many other tasks that are now completed using computers.

Examiner tip

You must make sure you can fully explain why each of these skills and qualities is valued by an employer.

Employers also value employees who are:

- reliable
- trustworthy
- honest
- disciplined
- motivated
- hard working
- co-operative
- sociable
- organised.

Why employers value these skills and qualities

Revised

Employers want employees who can deal with customers and clients in a professional manner. This leads to customers being satisfied with how they are treated and wanting to use the services offered by that company again, which will lead to increased profit.

Examiner tip

Learn the qualities/skills but ensure you learn this explanation as it can be applied to many of the skills and qualities.

How to cope with working part time and studying

Revised

The following strategies can help people cope with the stress of working part time and studying:

- Plan your time well so that there is a balance between work and study.
- De-stress by making time for social activities like going out with friends or physical training.
- If you are balancing a part-time job with full-time education, remember that you need to devote more time to studying.
- Find out about the possibility of study leave from your job during exam time.

The advantages and disadvantages or working part time and studying

Revised

Advantages	Disadvantages
• Earning money • Gaining independence from a parent/ guardian • A sense of achievement • Learning what it is like to be in a work environment • Meeting new people	• Finding the time for work • Finding the time for study • Finding the time for social activities • Balancing work and study

Test yourself

Tested

1 What skills and qualities are valued by employers?
2 What could you do if you were feeling stressed by working part time and studying?

3 What are the good points about getting a part-time job?

Answers online

Exam practice

Tested

Identify and explain the importance of demonstrating commitment in the workplace. *(2 marks)*

Answers online

The application process

What you need to know:
- The methods used to research a job or career
- How careers teachers can help with the career decision making process
- How the application process works
- Why employers use application forms
- How to complete an application form
- What should be included on a Curriculum Vitae (CV)
- How an employer chooses the applicants to interview
- Why interviews are used to fill job vacancies
- How to prepare for an interview or presentation
- How to perform at an interview or presentation
- Other methods used by an employer during the application process

Key terms

Job vacancy – an unfilled position with a company

Job advertisement – an announcement that a job is available, outlining the key competencies, qualities and experience required

Job description – a statement setting out the duties of a particular job

Job specification – a statement setting out the qualities and skills required of a potential employee

The methods used to research a job or career

Revised ☐

- Internet and careers programmes, e.g. JED (Job Explorer Database), Odyssey and Pathfinder
- Searching for information on the internet
- Discussion with careers teacher/learning for life and work teacher/form teacher/subject teacher
- A careers interview with the Careers Service
- Work experience in your chosen career
- Researching courses in your local higher and further education colleges (online or printed prospectus).

How careers teachers can help with the career decision making process

Revised ☐

- **Advice** – information about your chosen career path or possible courses at Institutes of Further and Higher Education
- **Mock interview** – a practice interview
- **Work experience** – help finding work experience in a sector in which you are interested
- **Curriculum Vitae (CV)** – help and advice to fill this in
- **Careers conventions** – outside conventions or those hosted at your school (provide further guidance and advice).

How the application process works

When employers recruit new employees they want to find the **perfect person** for the job:

Presentable   Perceptive
Efficient   Enthusiastic
Reliable   Resourceful
Full of energy   Stable
Educated   Organised
Careful   Negotiator
Tactful

> **Examiner tip**
>
> You must be able to identify and explain how the application process can allow an employer to assess your skills and qualities.

There is a series of processes that employers use to fill a job vacancy:

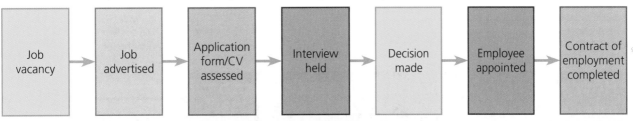

Job vacancy → Job advertised → Application form/CV assessed → Interview held → Decision made → Employee appointed → Contract of employment completed

Why employers use application forms

A prospective employer can get an insight into all your skills and qualities from the information you write in your application form. The form requests all the information that the business needs to know. All applicants provide the same information in the same order on the form and this makes it easier for the employer to compare applicants.

How to complete an application form

- Write clearly and accurately.
- Complete all sections.
- Write in blue or black ink.
- Sign and date the form.
- Check that all details are correct.
- Read over the form before you submit it to make sure there are no errors.
- Keep a copy of what you have written.

Make sure you read over your copy of the application before the interview – to remind yourself of what you wrote and in order to be prepared for any questions that might be asked about it.

What should be included on a Curriculum Vitae (CV)

Revised

A CV is a clear, brief and interesting way of presenting your personal profile. It is a personally designed document that sets out the main details about you.

What should be included on a CV	Why this should be included on a CV
Personal details	To identify yourself and allow the employer to contact you.
Education, qualifications and training	To allow the employer to see if you have the correct qualifications and skills for the job.
Work experience	This allows the employer to see if you are an experienced employee and gives them an insight into your previous work to see if you have the right knowledge and skills for the job.
Skills	This allows the employer to see any other skills that may be advantageous for the post applied for, e.g. if you can drive.
Interests and hobbies	This allows the employer to see the type of person you are and whether your interests match the job you are interested in.
References	This is a confidential statement from a person who will outline your strengths and state whether or not they consider you suitable for the job.

How an employer chooses the applicants to interview

Revised

Once an employer has received all the application forms, he or she will place them into three categories in order to choose which applicants to interview:

1. **Those to reject** – they did not meet the requirements set out in the job specification
2. **Those to place on a shortlist** – three to ten of the best applicants who are asked to interview
3. **Those to place on a long list** – some applicants may not be rejected immediately but kept on a long list in case one of the applicants in the short list drops out.

> **Examiner tip**
>
> You must be able to explain how an employer selects the applicants to be interviewed.

> **Examiner tip**
>
> It is important that you can identify and explain reasons why an interview is important to an employer and an applicant.

Why interviews are used to fill job vacancies

Revised

- **Suitability** – the **employer** gets a chance to meet the applicant and see if they are suitable for the job. The employer can assess, for example, the applicant's conversational ability.
- **Opportunity** – it is an opportunity for an **applicant** for show that they are the best person for the job, for example showing their enthusiasm.

- **Questions** – the **employer** can test the applicant's knowledge and skills to see whether they are the right person for the job and verify the information on the application form. All applicants are asked the same questions and given the same time, which allows the employer to compare the applicants. Questions may be asked about personal qualities and applicants may have to sit a test to ascertain their literacy or numeracy levels.

- **Appearance** – the **employer** can check the applicant's physical appearance so it is important that applicants dress respectably in neat and tidy clothes in order to create a good impression and show that they are worthy of getting the job. Appearance is particularly important in some businesses where the applicant will be representing the business and will be expected to dress appropriately in order to convey a good image.

- **Information** – it gives the **applicant** an opportunity to find out about working conditions, hours of pay, salary, training and promotion prospects. Applicants also get a chance to judge the business and friendliness of existing staff and see the facilities available.

How to prepare for an interview or presentation

Revised

- Find out about the business and the employer – what does the business do? Is it big/small? Is it a new/old business? Try to get an understanding of the business.

- Think about yourself – what skills are you good at? What qualities make you special? What qualities and skills make you employable? What about you would impress an employer?

- Find out where the interview is being held – plan your journey. How long will it take? How will you get there? Try to arrive ten minutes before the interview is due to begin to compose yourself.

- Think about what you will wear – does the clothing give off the right signals? Does your clothing show that you are respectable? Are your clothes neat and tidy?

- Organise your record of achievement/progress file – is everything in order? Is it up to date? Is it clean and not scruffy?

- Have a practice interview – what sort of questions will the interviewer ask? How will you answer them? What questions could you ask the interviewer?

- Practise your presentation – make sure any electrical equipment is operating properly, have a back-up USB with your presentation/notes.

How to perform at an interview or presentation

Revised

- Try not to be too nervous – be pleasant to the receptionist, the interviewer(s) and anyone else you meet; you want to give the right impression.

- Behave in an appealing way – sit up straight, be polite, be positive, smile, listen carefully, speak clearly, make eye contact.

- Answer the questions as best you can – use personal experience to explain a point, show interest, be keen.

- Ask a question(s) related to the job/business – show your knowledge.

- Keep your presentation to the time limit – have a good closing statement that sums everything up.

> **Examiner tip**
>
> You must be able to identify and explain how you could prepare for an interview and the ways to perform best in an interview.

Other methods used by an employer during the application process

Revised

Method used by an employer during the application process	Why this process is used
Letter or email correspondence	This allows an employer to judge your literacy skills and possibly ICT skills. This can also be in the form of a covering letter to accompany a CV. It should encourage the employer to want to know more about the person applying for the job.

Method used by an employer during the application process	Why this process is used
Telephone conversation	An employer could make a judgement on your motivation, social and flexibility skills. Telephones can be used to have an informal chat, set up an interview, carry out an interview or offer a person a job.
Mini assessment, e.g. presentation	An employer could carry this out during an interview to see if you have the suitable skills and qualities, e.g. dealing with a customer or using ICT to make a PowerPoint presentation.

Test yourself

Tested

1 List five ways to research a job or career.
2 Explain one reason why you should research a job or career.
3 What is a CV?
4 How does an employer choose who to short list for an interview?
5 List four reasons why employers like to interview people.
6 List two reasons why an employee might like to be interviewed.
7 List two ways you can prepare for an interview.
8 Write out four important ways to prepare for an interview.

Answers online

Exam practice

Tested

Identify and explain two ways a career teacher can help students make career decisions.

(4 marks)

Answers online

3.3: Rights and responsibilities of employers and employees

What are rights and responsibilities?

What you need to know:
● The responsibilities of an employer to employees
● What is included in a contract of employment
● The laws that protect employees' rights

Key terms

Duty of care – the responsibility that an organisation has towards its employees

Responsibilities – things that it is your job or duty to do

Rights – claims and privileges we expect to have

Salary – amount paid for one year's work, divided equally over twelve months

Wage – amount paid by the hour (often paid weekly)

The responsibilities of an employer to employees

Revised

	Employees' rights	Employers' responsibilities
Salary	To be paid fairly and on time for the work they do	To ensure employees are paid a fair wage on time and to ensure each employee is paying income tax and National Insurance

	Employees' rights	Employers' responsibilities
Career development	To have the opportunity for promotion	To ensure there are opportunities for career progression or promotion
Health and safety	To be safe at work	To ensure employees are fully trained in the use of all equipment in the workplace; to ensure all employees receive health and safety training; to follow health and safety legislation
Compassionate leave	To be shown consideration for personal matters	To allow unpaid time for family emergencies including funerals, as agreed in the terms and conditions of employment
Holidays	To have holidays	To ensure that all employees are allocated annual leave for holidays

What is included in a contract of employment

Revised

A contract of employment should include information about:

- your conditions, including annual holidays, annual sickness benefit and maternity/paternity leave
- your pay
- overtime
- the period of notice required.

The contract of employment is a legal document to protect your rights as an employee. It is a responsibility of the employer to ensure that all employees have a contract of employment.

The laws that protect employees' rights

Revised

Legislation has been passed by the government to make sure employees' rights are protected (see table below). It includes equality legislation that attempts to remove discrimination from the workplace, ensuring equality in gender, race, disability, etc. This equality legislation applies to all recruitment and selection procedures. The most vulnerable people in society are protected by these rights.

> **Examiner tip**
>
> You must be able to identify and explain how each piece of legislation protects employees' rights.

Law	Employees' rights	Employers' responsibilities
Equal Pay Act (NI) 1970	Men and women must be paid the same amount if they are doing a job of 'equal value'.	Must ensure that all employees are paid equally if they are doing jobs of 'equal value'.
Sex Discrimination (NI) Order 1976	Men and women must have equal treatment and opportunity in the workplace.	Must ensure that no one is discriminated against because of their gender.
Race Relations (NI) Order (2003)	People of all races, colours, nationalities and ethnic origins must be treated equally.	Must ensure that no one is discriminated against because of their race.
Disability Discrimination Act 1995	Able bodied, disabled and some people with mental impairments must be given the same opportunities.	Must ensure that no one with a disability is discriminated against.
Health and Safety at Work (NI) Order (1978)	All employees must be allowed to carry out their work in a safe environment.	Must ensure a safe working environment.
National Minimum Wage Act (1998)	All employees depending on their age must receive a minimum hourly wage.	Must ensure that employees are paid a minimum hourly wage.
Working Time Regulations (NI) order (1998)	This covers things such as holiday entitlement, the maximum hours an employee is expected to work, rest break entitlement, rest periods between working days and nights and Sunday working hours.	Workers over eighteen are generally entitled to: – 20–25 days' holiday per year (not including bank holidays) – a 20-minute break if the shift is longer than six hours – work no more than six days out of every seven, or twelve out of every fourteen days – work a maximum of 48 hours per week.

Law	Employees' rights	Employers' responsibilities
Employment Act (2002)	– Parents of children under six or with a disabled child under eighteen are allowed to ask to work flexibly. – Fathers can have two weeks of paid paternity leave (paid at the same rate as statutory maternity pay) within eight weeks of birth or placement of a new child. – Parents adopting a new child will receive the same leave as given for maternity leave (where possible).	– Employers must take any requests for flexible working seriously.

Test yourself

Tested ☐

1 What is a salary?
2 List the areas where an employer has a duty of care to an employee.
3 What is a contract of employment?

4 Name the legislation that means people of all races must be treated equally.
5 Name the legislation that means fathers can have two weeks' paternity pay.

Answers online

Exam practice

Tested ☐

Explain one reason why it is important that an employer explains where the fire exits are. *(2 marks)*

Answers online

Role of trade unions

What you need to know:
● The role of the trade union
● The advantages and disadvantages of belonging to a trade union for an employee
● The advantages and disadvantages of staff belonging to a trade union for an employer

Key terms

Shop steward – a person elected by workers to represent them in dealings with management

Strike – a refusal to work organised by a body of employees as a form of protest

Picket line – a boundary established by workers on strike, usually at the entrance to the place of work, that others are asked not to cross

Work to rule – a form of protest in which workers slow the rate of work by doing only the minimum amount required by the rules of the workplace

Go-slow – a form of protest in which work or progress is delayed or slowed down

The role of the trade union

Revised

- **To protect rights** – ensures rights of employees are protected in the workplace. Trade unions work to defend these rights.
- **To give advice** – gives advice and information to members about issues relating to their employment (holiday pay, sick pay, etc.).

- **To resolve conflict** – if employees are unhappy about something relating to the workplace trade unions will step in and work as mediators to resolve any issues.
- **To negotiate** – negotiates between employees and employers over issues such as pay and working conditions; works to rectify a problem.

The advantages and disadvantages of belonging to a trade union for an employee

Revised

Advantages of being a trade union member

- A trade union protects the rights of employees.
- If an employee is unhappy about pay and conditions they can ask a trade union representative to speak to the employer on their behalf.
- A trade union will work as a mediator between employers and employees to ensure staff are treated fairly.
- Trade unions can organise action to put pressure on an employer to make changes, e.g. strike (short or all-out), go-slow, work to rule or picket line.
- An employee can get advice and support from their trade union representative.
- If an employee has an issue they can ask their trade union representative to come with them to speak to management about the issue – negotiate on their behalf.
- If an employee has a question regarding their contract of employment, they can ask their trade union to clarify it.
- If an employee feels that their rights have been breached they can seek advice from their trade union which will investigate any problems they might have.
- A trade union will make sure there is career progression for employees.

Disadvantages of being a trade union member

- There is a membership fee, so if an employee never uses the services it can be seen as a waste of money.
- If a situation is not resolved, the trade union will take a vote on further action, e.g. strike. If the employee disagrees with this they may feel pressured into being involved.
- If staff take any industrial action this will disrupt production (loss of productivity). Employees will then have to catch up on work when they return after the strike action.
- Employees do not get paid while they are striking and this can have a serious impact on families and households. Furthermore, employees are not entitled to government benefits if they are on strike.
- Strike action can cause serious stress, depression and financial worries for employees.

Examiner tip

You must be able to explain the advantages and disadvantages to the employer *and* employee. Read the question carefully to see from which perspective you must write your answer.

3.3: Rights and responsibilities of employers and employees

The advantages and disadvantages of staff belonging to a trade union for an employer

Revised

Some employers will encourage their employees to join a trade union while others will not.

Advantages to employers of their staff being trade union members

- Employers can deal with the shop steward, the representative of the union in the workplace, instead of a number of different employees.
- Employers only need to distribute information to trade unions, which then pass it on to members.

Disadvantages to employers of their staff being trade union members

- Can encourage members to go against the company's wishes.
- Industrial action can give a company a negative reputation, which could affect orders and money coming into the business.
- Industrial action from the whole staff can result in profit losses for the company.
- Trade unions can force employers to increase wage rates and improve other terms and conditions.

Test yourself

Tested

1 List the main roles of a trade union.
2 List as many reasons as you can for an employee wanting to join a trade union.
3 Why would an employer not want their employees to become trade union members?
4 What industrial action can a trade union organise?
5 What are the consequences of this industrial action on a business?

Answers online

Exam practice

Tested

Evaluate the value for an employee of being part of a trade union.

(10 marks)

Answers online

The responsibilities that an employee has to an employer

What you need to know:
- The responsibilities of employees to their employers
- The importance of employees' responsibilities in the workplace
- The consequences of employees failing to meet their responsibilities
- The rewards for employees who continually meet their responsibilities

The responsibilities of employees to their employers

Revised

Employers' rights – to expect:	Employees' responsibilities – to make sure employers' rights are met by:
• loyalty and commitment • honesty • good attendance and punctuality • deadlines to be met	• putting in 100% effort • being truthful and trustworthy • attending work on time, every day • managing time and looking for help when needed

Examiner tip

You must be able to identify and explain why each of these responsibilities is important.

The importance of employees' responsibilities in the workplace

Revised

- **Loyalty** – employees should be loyal to their employer or the company they work for. Employees who work to the best of their abilities have high productivity levels, which can influence profit levels. They promote the good reputation of the company, which can attract new customers.

- **Honesty** – employees should be honest in all their dealings with colleagues and customers. Their employer should be able to trust them to handle valuable items and money. This gives employees confidence and encouragement to be a better employee. Being honest also ensures there is no theft of goods, which could result in a loss of profit for a company and a feeling of low morale among staff.

- **Health and safety** – employees must ensure their own safety and the safety of others. This will result in fewer accidents, which can cause damage to a company's reputation. If employees are off sick due to injury, there are lower levels of production.

- **Time keeping** – employees should be on time for work. It is essential for employees to be at work on time to carry out their duties. This ensures high productivity levels and customer satisfaction. If an employee is late for work, a colleague may have to cover for them and this creates negative feeling in the workplace, which can lead to reduced levels of production.

- **Meeting deadlines** – if deadlines are met, work will be produced on time which leads to customer satisfaction and a good reputation for the company and ultimately good profit levels.

- **Professionalism** – employees must act professionally in the workplace. This ensures that there is a level of respect and a good atmosphere in which to work. A good reputation will encourage staff to apply to work in the company. It will also attract customers if they know they will receive a professional service.

The consequences of employees failing to meet their responsibilities

Revised

If employees fail to meet their responsibilities, this can be seen as a breach of their contract of employment and disciplinary action can be taken. The action taken will depend on the seriousness of the breach.

1. **Verbal warning** – e.g. as a result of being late for work on a few occasions
2. **Written warning** (an employee may receive more than one of these depending on the employer's policy) – e.g. as a result of missing an important deadline
3. **Dismissal** – e.g. as a result of stealing or receiving a few written warnings.

An employee may also be forced to **retrain** in a particular area or be forced to **attend counselling**.

> **Examiner tip**
>
> You should be able to identify and explain the consequences for employees who do not meet their responsibilities as outlined in their contract of employment

> **Examiner tip**
>
> You should be able to explain how an employer can reward employees for meeting their responsibilities.

The rewards for employees who continually meet their responsibilities

Revised

Just as employees can be disciplined for breaching their contract of employment and not meeting their responsibilities, employees who continually meet their responsibilities can be rewarded both financially and non-financially.

Financial rewards

- **Bonus** – an extra payment for meeting targets or deadlines
- **Commission** – an employee may receive a percentage of the revenue they bring into the business through sales
- **Profit sharing** – some businesses sell shares to an employee at a discounted rate to give them ownership of the company.

Non-financial incentives

- **Recognition/status** – employees may be recognised for their efforts, e.g. as 'employee of the month', through recognition in a staff newsletter or by entering them in external competitions
- **Empowerment** – employees may be given more responsibility and authority to make decisions
- **Job enrichment** – employees may be given more interesting, challenging and more complex tasks
- **Job enlargement** – employees may be given more tasks to do, leading to more responsibility and greater variety of work
- **Consultation** – employers may take time to find out their employees' views and be willing to discuss their suggestions.

Test yourself
Tested ☐

1 What are the responsibilities an employee has to an employer?
2 Explain why each of these responsibilities is important.
3 What are the disciplinary actions an employer can take when an employee fails to meet their responsibilities?
4 List the financial rewards employees can be given when they continually meet their responsibilities.
5 What are the non-financial rewards employees can be given when they continually meet their responsibilities?

Answers online

Exam practice
Tested ☐

Explain one reason why it is important for an employee to meet deadlines.

(2 marks)

Answers online

How can businesses become more socially aware?

What you need to know:
- Why a business should be socially aware
- How businesses can address environmental issues
- Why a business should be concerned about environmental issues
- How climate change can impact on a business
- The impact of inner city renewal on employment

Key terms

Corporate Social Responsibility (CSR) policy – a policy covering areas such as the impact a business has on the local and global environment, consumers, employees and other stakeholders

Socially aware – examining decisions and growth in the light of the environment that a business operates in, on a local or global scale

Why a business should be socially aware
Revised ☐

Nowadays we are much more aware of the effects of our actions on the environment. This knowledge and awareness is influential when we buy goods as we prefer those that are environmentally friendly and from companies that are socially responsible. Businesses must therefore be aware of the effects of their actions on the environment and strive to be socially aware. They might do this by employing ethical strategies in the workplace and being involved in local projects and charity work.

How businesses can address environmental issues

Revised

Reducing	• Using email instead of postal mail within the workplace • Creating less packaging • Printing on both sides of the paper • Turning off lights and computers overnight
Reusing	• Purchasing reusable materials for the workplace, e.g. refurbished furniture and equipment • Refilling ink cartridges
Recycling	• Recycling tins, paper and plastic • Setting up recycling points • Making their products recyclable
Mitigating (lowering) greenhouse gas emissions	• Using energy efficient fuels/machinery to reduce the emission of the three main greenhouse gases (carbon dioxide, methane, nitrous oxide) • Using renewable energy sources such as wind turbines • Reducing electricity and heating demands • Using trains and buses rather than cars • Recycling to reduce land fill

Examiner tip

You need to be able to identify and explain how a business can become more socially aware of environmental issues.

Why a business should be concerned about environmental issues

Revised

An active environment interest by a business can be used to:

★ attract more customers (especially those who are socially responsible)
★ gain more profit from the extra customers spending their money
★ create new jobs, if the business becomes more popular it will need more staff
★ encourage potential employees to apply for jobs because they are interested in the environment too
★ help build a caring and socially aware corporate image
★ save money by reusing, reducing and recycling.

How climate change can impact on a business

Revised

Extreme weather conditions	Floods, hurricanes and other extreme weather conditions can damage property and disrupt the business.
Drought	Lack of water will affect businesses that rely on water for manufacturing such as farms. Lack of water also has an impact on health and safety in businesses.
Poorer air quality	This can lead to air pollution, which will have an impact on employees and animals.
Colder winters/ hotter summers	This leads to higher energy costs because of heating and air conditioning requirements.

Many scientists believe that greenhouse gases have contributed to global warming which causes climate change. Therefore, to be socially responsible, businesses and individuals need to reduce the amount of greenhouse gases produced.

The three main greenhouse gases are:

- carbon dioxide – comes from burning fossil fuels such as oil and coal
- methane – comes from rotting vegetation and landfills
- nitrous oxide – comes from fertilisers, burning fuels and industrial production.

Examiner tip

This knowledge should help you to explain the ways in which a business can reduce its greenhouse gas emissions and why it should do this.

The impact of inner city renewal on employment

Revised

Inner city renewal is the development of neglected areas within a city. These areas are given government grants to improve their facilities, e.g. new shop fronts, improved car parking, improved pavements and roads, new road signs or new works of art or culture.

Positives effects on employment

- New businesses will open, e.g. supermarkets, creating new job opportunities.
- New facilities will require staff, creating new job opportunities.
- Refurbishment of shop fronts, parks, etc. will create job opportunities.

Negative effects on employment

- Large supermarkets are able to offer low-cost pricing, a bigger range and unlimited free parking. This strong competition means corner shops won't sell as many goods as they did previously, and therefore won't be as profitable and may not be able to afford staff wages, so jobs may be lost.
- Corner shops also create a sense of community, which can be wiped out by supermarkets.
- Some people feel that the demise of the local shop affects the health of the population's lowest earners as it can lead to a lack of food shops and services in rural and poor areas.

Corner shops are now trying to compete with supermarkets in terms of under-pricing or matching prices and promoting their convenience and sense of community. Some people are now shopping in their local shops to support them rather than going to the supermarkets.

Test yourself

Tested

1 What are the 3 Rs regarding the environment?
2 Describe one way a business could reduce.
3 Describe one way a business could reuse.
4 Describe one way a business could recycle.
5 What is climate change?
6 Name three ways in which climate change could have an impact on a business.
7 Identify one way in which a business could address climate change.
8 Give three reasons why a business would want to be seen as environmentally aware.
9 Give two examples of inner city renewal.
10 Give one benefit of inner city renewal.

Answers online

Exam practice

Tested

Explain why a person should be aware of environmental issues when setting up a new business. *(6 marks)*

Answers online

3.4: Issues of self-employment and sources of support

The advantages and disadvantages of being self-employed

What you need to know:
- The characteristics of a successful entrepreneur
- The importance of carrying out market research before setting up a business
- The advantages and disadvantages of owning your own business

Key terms

Entrepreneur – a person who has taken a risk in order to carry out a business venture (usually to start up a business)

Self-employment – working for yourself – being your own boss

The characteristics of a successful entrepreneur

Revised

- A hard worker – to ensure you can put the hours and effort into turning an idea into a business
- Focused – to have the vision to work towards achieving this goal
- Motivated – to keep going despite setbacks and to continue to drive forward
- Responsible – to act in such a way that people know they can trust you and maybe take a gamble and invest in your new business
- Able to take risks –
- Confident –

- Creative –
- Enthusiastic –
- Flexible –
- Determined to succeed –
- Able to learn from mistakes –
- Professional –
- Innovative –
- Able to communicate –
- Able to take criticism from clients/customers/staff –
- A leader –
- A manager –

Examiner tip

You must be able to identify and explain why each of these characteristics is necessary to be a successful entrepreneur. Some examples have been done for you.

The importance of carrying out market research before setting up a business

Revised

An entrepreneur setting up a business needs to know:

- **if their product will sell well** so they know if there is a demand/need for their product/service that could lead to a business with a strong customer base
- **what the customer needs** so they know what service, quality or experience customers expect and can then cater appropriately for their customers

- **what the competition is** so they will be aware of the other products they are competing with on the market, which will enable them to price competitively pricing in order to gain market share.

The advantages and disadvantages of owning your own business

Revised

Advantages

Financial	Non-financial
• You get the profits. • You get the money to reinvest in what you want, such as other businesses. • You can make lots of money from owning your own business, and so can afford a high quality lifestyle.	• You are in control, and you are your own boss. You don't have to answer to a superior and you make the decisions. • You can work when you want to and so make your work fit around your family or lifestyle. • You will have the satisfaction of working on something you feel passionately about. • Running a successful business will boost your confidence and self-esteem.

Disadvantages

Financial	Non-financial
• You may lose the money that you have invested in the business. • You may have difficulty with cash flow (money coming in and out of a business), which affects your own personal finances. • You have to deal with the ebbs and flows of the economy – your business may be affected by a poor economic climate.	• You may not be an expert in all areas of running a business. • You are the only person responsible for the business and the staff. • You may need a lot of motivation. • You are responsible for carrying out the market research so if it goes wrong, this is your problem. • The amount of time and effort needed can have an impact on other areas of your life. You may come to dislike the business you loved. • You could end up with high levels of stress and worry. • If there are high levels of competition or not enough customer demand for your business, you may fail.

Test yourself

Tested

1 What does it mean to be self-employed?
2 What are the characteristics of an entrepreneur?
3 Give three reasons why you should carry out market research before setting up a business.
4 What might happen if you did not carry out market research before setting up a business?
5 Give three advantages to owning your own business.
6 Give three risks to owning your own business.

Answers online

Exam practice

Tested

Explain one advantage of being self-employed. *(2 marks)*

Answers online

Examiner tip

You should practise writing out the points in the above table as one continuous piece of writing to ensure you can evaluate being self-employed.

Support provided by agencies for self-employment

What you need to know:
- The sources of finance for the self-employed
- The sources of support for the self-employed

The sources of finance for the self-employed

Revised

- Bank loan
- Investment from other business people
- European Union
- Government
- Invest NI
- The Prince's Trust.

The sources of support for the self-employed

Revised

There are also various agencies that can offer support to self-employed people (see table overleaf).

Examiner tip

You must be able to identify and explain the role of each of the agencies in the table on page 100 and how they offer assistance to people who are self-employed.

Test yourself

Tested

1 List three places where you can get finance from if you are setting up a business.
2 Explain two ways DEL helps those who want to be self-employed.
3 What particular areas does DETI give guidance on?
4 Give three examples of assistance offered by The Prince's Trust.
5 Name a programme which Invest NI provides to give support to business.
6 Give an example of the work that Enterprise NI does.

Answers online

Exam practice

Tested

Name two organisations that give help and support to self-employed people in Northern Ireland. *(2 marks)*

Answers online

Agencies that provide support for the self-employed

Agency	Role	Support provided	How?	Examples of assistance	Websites
DEL (Department for Employment and Learning)	Helps people to get new skills and provides guidance to those who want to be self-employed	• Steps to Work Programme for those who are 18+ (or 16+ and a lone parent) and unemployed • Graduate Acceleration Programme (GAP)	Opportunities to retrain, get qualifications and work experience under the guidance of an adviser	• Work placements • Qualifications • Personal adviser	www.delni.gov.uk
DETI (Department of Enterprise, Trade and Investment)	Helps to decide and deliver government policy on areas such as Tourism, Social Economy and Enterprise	Mostly through Invest NI (see below) but can offer guidance for self-employed people in various different areas	Guidance on areas around: • Tourism • Innovation (new ideas) • Energy • Global markets • Health and Safety	• A place to go if you need information on any of the areas listed to the left • It has policies and statistics that entrepreneurs may find useful when researching or conducting business	www.detini.gov.uk
The Prince's Trust	Helps young people aged 18–30 who are unemployed to start up in business	Advice on: • Employment options that are available • Business training • Business planning • Funding guidance from a mentor	Downloadable guides with help in the following areas: • Business planning • Finding premises • Sales and marketing • Managing finances • Legalities • Taxation • Business behaviour	• 24-hour helpline • Virtual office space • Online accounting system • Web designing • Town and country market opportunities to sell products or services • Money grants	www.princes-trust.org.uk
Invest NI	Part of DETNI – gives advice and assistance to new and existing businesses on starting up or growing their business domestically or internationally. Attracts new business to NI	Go For It programme and Growth programme offer advice on exporting and global trading and encourage foreign investment to set up in NI	Meetings, workshops and training seminars (on finance, planning, IT, marketing, design, etc.) • Mentoring support from experts • Business clinics where problems can be discussed and hopefully solved	• Personal business advisors • Training and workshops • One-to-one mentoring • Networking opportunities • Online support • Support to develop business plans • Offers grants • Organises international trade fairs	www.investni.com www.nibusinessinfo.co.uk
Enterprise NI	Represents the Local Enterprise Agencies in NI. These are independent, local, not-for-profit companies that try to help support small business development and encourage economic development activity in NI	Provides services for small businesses such as funding and information	• Guidance on grants and initiatives available to small businesses • Professional advice from experienced business people • Advice on programmes available to help businesses and entrepreneurs grow and develop	• Help with finding financial assistance in a particular area • Help with finding business accommodation • Help with new technologies • Help when using programmes such as Go For It (Invest NI)	Local Enterprise Agency Map can be found at www.enterpriseni.com